"GENTLEMAN" JOHN PERKINS

By W. W. Scott

———

———

Price $1.50

———

———

Published by

THE LENOIR NEWS-TOPIC

LENOIR, N. C.

INTRODUCTORY

These compilations do not assume the guise and dignity of history or biography, but are submitted as material that may be used by the exact historian after verification.

Born in 1733 and dying in 1804, John Perkins has been succeeded, during the 115 years following his death, by six generations of descendants, the progeny of five sons and two daughters, whose families in each generation have been prolific beyond the average. The principal "habitat" of the members of this family who have remained in North Carolina is comprised within the boundaries of the counties of Burke, Caldwell, Buncombe, Iredell, Catawba, Wilkes and McDowell, although they are to be found in nearly every county in the State. From time to time many of them have moved to other States, and they have been traced to every State in the Union except the New England States, and some of them may be there. It is probable that they could be found in considerable numbers as citizens of foreign countries, although Brazil is the only foreign country to which any of them has been traced as citizens. Thus scattered there are hundreds, perhaps thousands, of them living in the United States and in other countries, and yet the date and place of birth of John Perkins was known to few if any of these descendants before 1907, when it was first published. In one branch of the family the story was handed down, inaccurate as traditional statements are apt to be, that he was born in England, the son of a wealthy family, on intimate terms with the Earl of Granville, and that he was sent, as a youth, to North Carolina under the tutelage of a guardian who helped him to establish himself upon a valuable grant of lands made to him by the Earl of Granville. This tradition was disproved by the following publication made in the Lenoir Topic of June 7, 1911:

"I note with pleasure that Rev. J. H. Shuford is to write a series of local historical articles for the Topic, and I was especially interested in the first installment in the last number of the paper on John Perkins.

"The late Judge McCorkle of Newton wrote a series of articles concerning John Perkins and his family, which was published in the Newton Enterprise in 1883 and republished, with Judge McCorkle's permission, in the Topic on April 30 and May 7 and 14, 1890. Like Mr. Shuford, Judge McCorkle did not know from what section John Perkins came to North Carolina. I can inform you. Mrs. C. B. Harrison of Lenoir owns an old English prayer book which was the property of her great-great-grandfather, Parson Miller—Rev. Robert Johnstone Miller of blessed memory—and on one of the blank pages of this book is written in Mr. Miller's own hand the following:

"'John Perkins of Lincoln county, State of North Carolina, son of Elisha Perkins, of the State of Virginia, was born in Virginia, on the fifteenth day of September, 1733, A. D., and departed this mortal life on Friday morning at five minutes past 7 o'clock, the thirteenth day of April, 1804, aged 70 years and 7 months, wanting 2 days.'

"I think it probable that Elisha Perkins was a citizen of Frederick county, Virginia, which in those days covered a large part of the Valley of Virginia. Winchester is the capital of the present smaller county of Frederick, as it was of the older and larger Frederick. Stannard's 'Virginia Colonial Register' reports that in the Virginia Assembly of 1752-5, sessions of August 22, 1754, May 1, 1755, and October 27, 1755, Frederick county was represented by George William Fairfax and ———— Perkins. The journals of the Virginia Assembly of that date are concisely written, making little reference to members except those belonging to committees. In the proceedings of Wednesday, May 21, 1755, is this record: 'Ordered, That Mr. Perkins have leave to be absent from the service of this House for the remainder of this session.' In the Dinwiddie papers Governor Dinwiddie makes a number of references to having advanced to Mr. Perkins 500 pounds for the purchase of flour for the army, engaged about 1750 in holding the French and Indians at bay, but refers to him simply as 'Mr. Perkins.'

"These facts are derived from an article written for the Baltimore Sun of Dec. 8, 1907, which states further: 'John Perkins was born in Frederick county, Virginia, in 1733, the son of Elisha Perkins, and removed to North Carolina in 1751 or 1752. This would make Elisha Perkins, father of John Perkins, of an age between the minimum of 40 and the maximum of 50 years in 1752, eligible in age to represent Frederick county in the Assembly of 1752-5.'

"No record has yet been discovered that shows what was the given name of ———— Perkins, who served in the Colonial Assembly of 1752-5 as one of the representatives of Frederick county. The Baltimore Sun's writer makes a plausible, though not conclusive, argument in favor of Elisha Perkins as the man.

"One incident not generally known in the life of Parson Miller (who married John Perkins' daughter, Mary, and resided at Mary's Grove, two and a half miles west of Lenoir) is that he took part in political as well as in religious matters. He was one of the delegates from Burke county to the Constitutional Convention that met at Hillsboro in 1788. (See N. C. State Record.)   W. W. SCOTT."

Following is the communication published in the Baltimore Sun of Dec. 8, 1907:

"Stannard's excellent publication, the 'Virginia Colonial Register,' reports that in the Virginia Assembly of 1752-55, sessions of August 22, 1754, May 1, 1755, and October 27, 1755, Frederick county was represented by George William Fairfax and ———— Perkins. In the Dinwiddie papers Governor Dinwiddie makes a number of references to having advanced to Mr. Perkins £500 for the purchase of flour for the army, but always refers to him simply as 'Mr .Perkins.' I would like to know the given name of Representative Perkins.

"In the Assembly of 1775-6, session of June 1, 1775, and in the conventions of March 20, 1775, and of December 1, 1775, Pittsylvania county was represented by Peter Perkins and Benjamin Lankford. Was this Peter Perkins a son or connection of ———— Perkins of the Assembly of 1752-55?

"The history of John Perkins, of North Carolina, may assist in the discovery of the given name of Representative Perkins, of Frederick. John Perkins was born in Frederick county, Virginia, in 1733, the son of Elisha Perkins, and removed to North Carolina in 1751 or 1752. This would make Elisha Perkins, father of John, of an age between the minimum of 40 years and the maximum of 55 years in 1752, eligible in age to represent Frederick in the Assembly of 1752-55.

"Stannard says that in the eighteenth century the Burgesses in Virginia were paid their salaries by the counties through the instrumentality of the levy courts at their meetings, following the sessions of the Assembly, for attendance upon which pay was asked. There are, perhaps, records at Winchester that would throw light upon the given name of ———— Perkins."

The writer of this paper from childhood up to comparatively recent years had the most meagre information regarding the history of John Perkins, his great-great-grandfather, which may be summed up in his understanding that his ancestor was a fine old gentleman, a good citizen of some prominence in Lincoln county, very hospitable, a man of wealth in horses, cattle and many acres of fertile land, with plenty of servants around him. He really knew little more than this about John Perkins except that there were many other men, women and children with whom he came in contact who also claimed descent from John Perkins and who knew little more about their ancestor than he did. So he placed his great-great-grandfather in a category with Adam and Noah and was content to trace his lineage in a general way from these three worthies. Of course this dense ignorance did not apply to the older generations of John Perkins descendants, but only to most of the present and perhaps the immediately preceding generations.

Not until 1890 did this mist of ignorance begin to lift from the present writer, who in that year, chanced to run across Judge McCorkle's account (published in the Newton Enterprise in 1883) of the marriage of Col. Ephraim Perkins and Betsy Abernethy, and republished in the Lenoir Topic. It was delightful reading and was the inspiration for research for the collection of records, publications, family histories and traditions, kept up from that day to this, that has resulted in the following compilations, which are submitted for what they are worth. Judge McCorkle's contribution, aside from the interesting and charming story that it carries, is of historical value and will add to the interest of these pages. It has therefore been incorporated in the account which follows, certain inaccuracies which it contains being pointed out.

THE MARRIAGE OF EPHRAIM PERKINS AND ELIZABETH ABERNETHY

Col. M. L. McCorkle in Newton Enterprise, 1883.

I.

[Col. M. L. McCorkle, of Newton, has kindly permitted us to reprint the following sketches, first published in the Newton Enterprise in 1883. They are quite interesting and will occupy space in two or three issues of the paper. The first record we have of John Perkins was of his meeting with Bishop Spangenberg and being employed by him as a guide in his exploring expedition. That was in 1752 and John Perkins was just 19 years old. The Bishop had been advised to employ him by Andrew Lambert, "a well-known Scotchman." Adam Sherrill's son married Elizabeth Lowrance, a sister of John Perkins' wife, Catherine Lowrance.]

John Perkins immigrated to this country along with that great pioneer, Adam Sherrill, when he was a mere lad. Whether he was an orphan, or whether he was one of those daring, venturesome, go-ahead boys, that durst not like to brook control from parents or guardians, and left father and mother and kinsmen to seek his fortune in the wilds of North Carolina—we are only left to conjecture. When he arrived at full age he showed himself every inch a man. He acquired great wealth. He owned all that valuable country from the Island Ford, along the Catawba river to the mouth of Lysle's creek, several thousand acres, besides several thousand acres in Burke county, along the beautiful valley of John's river, from whom it took its name. He had great pride of ancestry. He believed in blood, both in men, horses and other live stock. He married Catherine Lowrance and settled on the western banks of the great Catawba not far from Little's Ferry. When Bishop Spangenberg made his tour of inspection in western North Caroolina for the purpose of locatnig lands for the Moravian settlements in 1752 he was living there then. The Bishop mentions his name and says: "I especially recommend John Perkins as a diligent and trustworthy man and a friend of the brethren." His house was so located that he could stand on his eastern porch, and from it look upon his broad acres of river bottom, and see his many servants at work or view his race horses make their four miles in the quickest time. He never allowed his blooded colts fed high or on grain till they arrived at four years of age. To feed them on corn injured their eyes, made them beefy and sluggish; but he never permitted them to become so thin in flesh as to make them crooked and out of shape. He raised some of the finest horses this country ever produced, both for speed, durability and long life.

He was blessed with five sons—Elisha, Ephraim, Eli, John, Joseph and Alexander. The two former inherited all their father's land in Catawba county, the three latter all the lands on John river. All the sons were large, handsome, well-proportioned men. Ephraim Perkins was about six feet high, complexion somewhat light, with blue eyes, finely chiseled nose, a massive forehead, and an intellectual face. He saw Elizabeth Abernethy. He fell in love at first sight. He did not resolve and resolve again what to do. He determined to offer her his hand and heart. Her father, David Abernethy, lived in what is now Lincoln county, about six miles southwest of Beatty's Ford, on a plantation now owned by Miss Sallie Lucky. The maiden name of her mother was Martha Turner. Her parents were from Virginia, but originally from Aberdeen, Scotland. She had six brothers, Robert, David, John, Turner, Moses and Miles, and two sisters, Nancy, who married Gen. Forney, and Martha, who married Robert Abernethy. Betsy was said to be the handsomest woman of her day. She was tall and handsome, and her form and moving was graceful and elegant. Her eyes were dark and sparkling, and her hair as black as the raven's wing; her cheeks were as the sunny side of the luscious peach; her lips somewhat pouting, challenging kisses. It was said that the Abernethys received their dark complexion from their Pocahontas blood. Whether this was said in envy or as a compliment we cannot tell. The Scotch-Irish blood cannot be enriched by that of any people on earth, especially not by the Indian race. The Scotch-Irish have shown themselves capable of meeting every emergency, in peace or war, in church or state, in the pulpit or forum, in every place of trust, honor or usefulness in this broad land. With the Scotch-Irish to plan and originate and go ahead and the German element to improve the lessons tought, this country is destined to be ,if not now, the foremost nation on earth.

The day was fixed for Ephraim Perkins and Betsy Abernethy to be married. A large number of friends were invited. It was about the year 1800. Then the country was prosperous and everything plentiful. The bridegroom and bride lived about twenty-five miles from each other. Everybody rode horseback in those days. No Jersey wagon or English gig had been introduced. A lady could then mount her well-caparisoned steed of dapple grey, chestnut sorrel or blood-red bay, with reins well drawn up, and move off with more grandeur and beauty than to be seated in a delicate phæton or gilded carriage. It was understood that a party from the bride would go out to meet the bridegroom on his way to the wedding, near Denver in Lincoln county, and there would be a trial of speed between the two parties. The prize was to be, who should have the honor of leading the bride in the first set in the dance. Everybody danced in those days. They did not think there was any harm in a social dance. When the bridal party approached near the place of meeting they sent out a company of videttes. They had not gone far till they saw in the distance the bridegroom's party coming. The videttes advanced within a few paces of the other party, saluted them, threw down the gauntlet and turned and flew back to their comrades. They were immediately pursued. The race was well maintained on both sides for some distance, but the blooded stock of the Perkinses outwinded the horses of the videttes and passed them, and the bridegroom's party obtained the prize.

The party soon arrived at the point proposed. A large number of invited guests were waiting to give them a hearty greeting. The negro servants ran far down the lane, ready to seize the reins of the spirited horses and lead them around to the well-stored racks of hay and troughs of corn and oats. It was an hour or two before Phebus should drive his golden chariot behind the western hills. The large grassy lawn in front of the house was covered with fair women and brave men, assembled on this festive occasion. The older men were talking politics—of the election of the elder John Adams to the presidency of the United States. The younger were engaged in athletic sports, as jumping with a long pole or leaping three jumps. The boys were in the rear of the house, near a straw stack, testing their early manhood in wrestling, either in back or waistband hold. Gen. Peter Forney was there. He had been a member of Congress from that district from 1794 to 1796. He was the husband of Nancy, oldest sister of the bride. He had just come from Washington city and was telling his neighbors and fellow citizens of George Washington's farewell address—that the whole house on its being read was bathed in tears. His son Daniel was there, a mere strapling. He had a peculiar mark—a white lock of hair on a black head, just above his forehead—born so. He afterwards became one of North Carolina's most distinguished sons. He represented her in Congress from 1815 to 1818. Robert Abernethy, the only brother of David Abernethy, was there. He had been the delegate from Tryon county to the Halifax congress, at which the North Carolina Bill of Rights was passed—the masterpiece of political statesmanship. John D. Abernethy, who had married Susan Mariah Forney, was there. He settled on a place on Mountain creek, called the John Abernethy forge place. He and Bartlett Shipp, that study patriot, big-brained, common-sense lawyer and strong advocate, were great friends, and had many a keen encounter of wits. On one occasion Mr. Shipp told Abernethy that he had an overseer (his name was John Fisher) that he desired to swap off. Abernethy having one of his own name, told him that he would swap. Neither knew the name of the other's overseer. Mr. Shipp said his was so lazy he would not work himself nor make any one else work, and he would swap for anybody in the world, except an Abernethy. This soft impeachment might be applied to some of the Abernethy men, but not the women, for they are all industrious and make good housewives. Turner Abernethy, who had married Dicey Abernethy, his cousin, was there. He was the most active man of his day. He could leap forty feet at three jumps —with a pole jump fifteen feet high. He is the father of Dixon, Sterling, Felix, Dr. T. M. Abernethy and Patsy, wife of Hiram Lowrance (the mother of M. E. Lowrance), and Nancy, who married John Perkins, and who is said to have been a paragon of beauty. There, too, was William Abernethy, the father of Albert, Pat, Drury, Joseph, David and Betsy. The latter married Albert Oglesby. Miles, the youngest brother of the bride, was then unmarried.

The minister, contrary to custom, was chosen by the bridegroom. His name was Robert Johnson Miller, who was an Episcopal clergyman. He had been ordained to preach by the Lutheran Synod, ex necessitate rei. He was the brother-in-law of the bridegroom, and at that time was pastor of upper and lower Smyrna churches in the eastern portion of Catawba county. The candles were lighted and the guests assembled in the large and spacious hall. The bridegroom and bride made their appearance with the attendants. The rites of matrimony were celebrated according to the Episcopal service. It was repeated in such a solemn and impressive manner as if it was intended that they should dwell together as husband and wife so long as they should live, and not in the light and trifling manner as is sometimes done in this age of divorces, when the marriage vow only lasts till the husband can find one more congenial to his vitiated tastes. After the wedding was over came the dinner—some called it supper—where was every luxury that taste could select or appetite suggest—enough for all, enough and to spare. After all had feasted the hall was cleared and a few sets—not the German, the racquet nor the square—but the old Virginia reel was danced, and all was over. First the bride disappeared, then the bridegroom—no one knew where.

II.

Happy is the bride the sun shines on. The sun rose beautifully clear. Not a cloud was to be seen above the horizon. Night's candles had gone out and darkness seemed to have fled the earth.

The birds were warbling their sweetest notes. The skipping lambs, the bleating sheep, the lowing herd, the chiming bells, the dense forest all gave interest to the scene. All nature seemed to rejoice and send up anthems of praise to the giver of every good.

The guests arose and, with the family, assembled in the large hall for the purpose of offering up their morning sacrifice, for our ancestors were a religious people. The Rev. Robert Johnston Miller conducted the services. All arose from bended knees and at the first call repaired to the well-filled table of smoking viands of venison and beefsteak and salad of wild turkey, snow-white biscuits or lightbread and buckwheat cakes well prepared, milk deep set with cream, and coffee of delicious aroma.

When all were served and breakfast over an invitation was again repeated to each and to all to accompany the happy pair to the reception. It was called "infare" then.

Then there was hurrying to and fro, to gather up the scattered articles of dress and place them in their reticules, for no saratogas were used in those days. Then were brought in front of the gate the well-trained and prancing horses. When the good-by was given they all mounted their prancing steeds and started on their happy voyage. Blossomed trees and waving corn and grassy plains were passed in review, with here and there a deer scampering over the plain.

At 12 o'clock they arrived at John D. Abernethy's, the brother of the bride. He had married Susan Maria Forney, as was said before. They lived on Mountain creek, not far from the eastern end of Anderson's mountain, in Catawba, not far from where Col. Francis Lock and his brave companions held a council of war the night before the battle of Ramsaur's mills. The wedding party stopped to take lunch. While there they heard the rising and swelling notes of music in the distance. All ears greeted the sound and all eyes were anxious to see the race. The sound came nearer and nearer. First they beheld the lord of the forest, a noble buck, with antlers raised high, bounding over the plain. Next came a well-trained pack of deer hounds pressing him hard. Abram Gabriel, who was fleet and quick of motion, ran for the rifle and jerked her down and found that she was not loaded. He filled the charger, poured down the powder, then next rammed down the bullet without patching, and took his stand. The game had passed by the admiring and anxious party. What disappointment! The noble stag had not gone far, till he turned and came back nearer than before. The sharp crack of the rifle was heard close by, and the stag at the report redoubled his speed as if he had a new lease of life, ran about 100 yards, fell stretched upon the plain.

John D. Abernethy and his wife, Susan Maria, were blessed with 12 living children. It is a blessing for one man to have so many children! There is no danger of his name not living forever and being forgotten. These children have all lived to be over three score and ten and all who have died were over four score except one who died at forty. They had six sons and six daughters. Of the daughters, Charity married William Young. Nancy married Thomas Rozzell. Polly married Abram Dailey. He died and she then married Absalom Duncan. Elizabeth Maria married Francis McCorkle and Susan married Alfred Hoke. The sons were Jacob, William, Miles W., David, Franklin and John B. Abernethy. The daughters were all fair to look upon and noble specimens of womanhood. The sons were rich with native intellects. Miles W. Abernethy was one of the noblest and best men that ever lived. He represented "old Lincoln" county in the Legislature two sessions, 1831 and 1833. At the last session an act was passed making the offices of the clerks of the counties and superior courts elective by the people instead of being appointed by the magistrates of the county. He was a man of great popularity. And although his primary education was limited, he became a man of great information. His manners were so gracious and so pleasing no one ever saw him that did not love him. And although of dark complexion, his noble, generous face, large dark brown eyes, his beaming countenance made him one of the handsomest men of his day. He became a candidate for the office of county court clerk in 1832. The then incumbent, Vardry McBee, was also a candidate. He was a man of rare accomplishments. He was never known to undertake anything or to engage in any enterprise that did not prosper in his hands. He had held the office a number of years. It had help to make him rich. He had discharged his duties honestly and faithfully and with skill and ability. Nothing could be said against this wonderfully successful man. Some said he had had it long enough. For the first time the word "rotation" in office was heard. The two were condidates. The old county was well canvassed by them, and also by John D. Hoke and John Coulter, who were candidates for the office of Superior Court clerk. There were no opposing politics at that day. All were Andrew Jackson men. Jackson had not removed the deposits then. The candidates ran more on their personal popularity than any question of State or national policy. The country became stirred up from circumference to center. The excitement was so great that it was preached in the churches. At Lincolnton on the evening of the election the returns came in very early. Mr. McBee led the ticket till late at night. His friends were jubilant. Music and dancing were heard. The flowing bowl and the joyous laugh ran high. Late in the night the sound of the hollow hoofs of horses were heard coming from the north of the county. There was a rush that way. "Hoke's box!" was the cry.

It had given Abernethy almost a unanimous vote. Old "Catfish" stood then together, as now. It elected Abernethy by several hundred. It was Abernethy's neighbors that did it! The one shout of triumph arose by his friends. Then all was hushed in silence. He filled the office for four years. In 1836 he left the State, as too many of North Carolina's most gifted sons have done, and settled in Jacksonville, Ala. He represented his county in the State Senate of Alabama with great credit and approbation for several terms and could have gone to Congress had he desired. He died only a few years ago, beloved and mourned by all who knew him. And the elements so mixed in him that Nature might stand up and say to the world, "This was a man."

Lunch being over, the party visited the falls of Moravian Creek and the iron works, owned by John D. Abernethy, which were in full blast, situated on that stream at that point.

Mountain creek rises out of the highest point on Anderson's mountain on the northwest side and runs northeast along the base of that mountain till it breaks through that range at the point above described, and turns its course and runs southeast and continues in that direction until it empties into the great Catawba near the Lincoln line. Leopard's creek rises out of the same mountain on the same side not far from the source of Mountain creek, and runs in an opposite direction from that stream, till it turns and bursts through that mountain range near Derr's furnace, then continues south till it unites with Anderson's creek, and the two make Dutchmen, which empties into the South Fork near Lineberger's cotton mills. Anderson's creek rises out of the same mountain not far from the source of the two others, but at the west end, at the celebrated mountain spring, where many a weary traveler quenched his parched thirst, and runs nearly due south until it unites with Dutchman creek, as before said. Along these mountain streams many boys and girls have grown up to man and womanhood that have and are playing well their parts in the great drama of life, and will live long as the good and great are revered by a grateful country. Anderson mountain is a continuation of the King's mountain range, which extends itself through Gaston, Lincoln and Catawba counties till it is broken up by the great Catawba at Buffalo shoals. This range runs parallel with the great Appalachian chain northeast and southwest. The highest points on this belt are King's, Crowder's and Anderson's mountains—the other portion having been washed in an early period of the world's history and shortly after the upheaval, and is comparatively a level country, and has left partly exposed on the northern edge of this range some of the richest gold deposits and gold-bearing veins of any place east of the Mississippi river, and tradition says that during the early history of this country silver and lead were found in great abundance in a little higher latitude on this same belt. Inexhaustible lime beds are found from King's mountain to the Catawba river along this range, and at one point—at A. D. Shuford's—a fine quality of marble. On the south side of this range vast beds of iron ore, both gray and magnetic, are found, and along this same belt are found vast deposits of graphite.

This range is only fifty miles in length, and, take it all in all, is probably the richest mineral belt for its length in the world, and yet it lacks want of capital, energy and labor.

Seventy-five years ago all along this mineral range the ring of the forge hammer and the crash of the rolling mills and roaring of the smelting furnaces of iron ore could be heard. Now all is hushed in silence.

There were giants in those days. The Forneys, the Brevards, the Grahams, the Abernethys and others like them lived and owned and worked on this vast mineral belt. And shall their descendants and those who are their successors be content to raise a patch of corn and cotton and live at this poor dying rate till some one of more energy and perseverance (probably from the North) shall come and "push them from their stools" and reap a rich golden harvest of wealth by developing these vast resources? No country can become rich and populous by producing the raw material alone. The most ordinary intellect is able to raise that. It is intellectual culture and skilled labor that man-

8

ufactures the costliest fabrics, and there the great profit lies. It is true that in this age capital is required to manufacture, but combinations can be formed and supply it where it does not exist otherwise. There are too many men engaged in buying and selling, and too few in converting the raw material into manufactured goods. The country is dwarfed, intellect is starved and genius is driven away, and then the country is dependent upon other people for the luxuries and even many of the necessaries of life.

From these reveries the party awoke and the cry was "To horse, to horse!" They all mounted their gaily steeds, and were soon on their journey to the hospitable home of Gentleman John Perkins, where a large number of anxious friends awaited their coming, and "whose eyes grew brighter when they came."

III.

The parents of Ephraim Perkins met the blushing bride at the gate and welcomed her and the guests to their hospitable home. The mother soon made her feel as one of the family. True politeness consists in making all around us feel pleasant and agreeable. Catharine, the noble wife of John Perkins, was an accomplished woman. She had been well bred. Her father was Isaac Lowrance, who lived at the Bunker Hill place in this county, and there he died and was buried. All the sons of John Perkins were there. Joseph, the oldest, was there. He had married Malissa Lavender and they were the parents of their elegant and accomplished daughter, Mira, who afterwards married George Conley, Esq., late of Caldwell county, and who are the ancestors of Mortimer Conley, Esq., and the grandmother of Judge Conley, of Iredell county. The Rev. Robert Johnston Miller and his most excellent wife, Mary, were there. Their son, Elisha P. Miller, the father of Caldwell county, and who represented Burke in the North Carolina Legislature from 1838 to 1840 and afterwards Caldwell county from 1846 to 1848 in the commons, and was one of the most useful men in his day—a true type of his old ancestor, "Gentleman John Perkins," was there. He is the father of Nelson Miller and the grandfather of W. W. Scott, editor of The Lenoir Topic.

John Perkins, Jr., was there. For the first time he beheld Nancy Abernethy. She was not more than sweet sixteen, was well grown and had blue eyes, and was fair as the lily. The winds of heaven had never been permitted to beteem her face too roughly. Her form was faultless, her moving elegant, her conversational powers unsurpassed for one of her age. Young as she was, she sighed and felt no pain. John Perkins and she gave to each other unutterable looks. They shortly afterwards were husband and wife, and they are the ancestors of Susan, consort of the late Richard Bichaux, of Burke county. Alfred Perkins, the father of Alexander and Robert Perkins, "Par nobile fratrum," was also there.

Alexander and Eli, two other sons of John Perkins, were also there. Eli never married. And although John Perkins was an aristocrat, yet his neighbors were all there. The preparations were large, the feast was rich. Everything was done to make all enjoy themselves. Some amused themselves in one way, some in another. Some promenading, some boat riding on the great Catawba. The most attractive sport of all was the race between the blooded colts (four in number) of John Perkins. They were all thoroughbreds or imported. There was one whose name was Peacock, because when he ran he curled his tail over his back. The colts were led out by their colored riders and grooms to the race ground, on the large bottom in front of the house. All eyes turned in that direction when the cry was given "The riders are up!" One of the colts became refractory, but was soon calmed down. The judges were seated high on a platform. The word was given and they all made nearly an even start. The goal before them was four miles. They seemed to be flying without wings. For the first mile they ran nearly in a breast. On and on they flew. Now bay Maria is ahead, then Peacock leads the race. Handkerchiefs began to wave. The excitement ran high. Now bets of tokens of love began to be made between the younger spectators of both sexes. Neither cared which would win. The last mile was now being repeated. There was a chestnut sorrel that had been led by the others. His name was Cuckleburr. He was of the Flying Childers stock. The last quarter he began to maintain his reputation. There was a shout for his success. As they passed the last pole he ran a little ahead. They had all done well. They were immediately blanketed and led away. The races were over, the entertainment ended and all felt grateful to "Gentleman John Perkins" for his kindness and hospitality.

Ephraim Perkins and his lovely bride spent their honeymoon visiting their friends. What married couple will ever forget their honeymoon —the primrose path of pleasure, peace, joy, ecstatis bliss! Not a care, not a wave of trouble disturbs their happy souls. After that they enter into a new life. They have to swarm out from the old hive. A new government must be established—often ruled by a queen. They would like to linger around the old homestead; but like the eagles, the eaglets must be pushed from their nests, their infant wings to try, and battle through the storms of life. They were settled on a plantation not far from the home of their childhood, now owned by M. J. Cochran. In the process of time they became the happy recipients of ten children—five sons and five daughters. The sons were Elisha, who married Linny Sherrill, his neighbor, Enos Sherrill's, daughter. David and Daniel died unmarried. John married Elizabeth Norris and Robert married Elzabeth Martin, who died, and he married her sister Matilda. The daughters were Adaline, who married Abel A. Shuford. Caroline married Colin Campbell, of Tennessee. Catharine married John Beard. Elizabeth married Dr. Robert Adams, and Martha, called Patsy, married

Hon. F. D. Reinhardt, who represented old Lincoln county from 1844 to 1850 in the North Carolina Legislature. Patsy was the youngest daughter. She was large, fine looking, dignified and of excellent manners. She was full of kindness and benevolence. She was a loving wife, an affectionate mother, a good neighbor and a devoted Christian. She loved her husband, her children, her kin and her God. She was baptized by her uncle, Rev. R. J. Miller, and afterwards confirmed by him—a member of the Episcopal Church, the church of her father; but when she married she joined the church of her husband, the Reformed Church. She considered that the four great reformed churches of the 16th century—the Anglican or Episcopal, the Lutheran, the German or Dutch Reformed and the Scotch Reformed or Presbyterian churches—were essentially the same in their main features—justification by faith and salvation by grace.

Hers and her husband's home was a great place of resort for the young people of the neighborhood—especially on festive occasions. One Christmas eve a party of young people paid them a visit. During the evening they engaged in several innocent amusements. They challnged each other before retiring that they would catch each other's Christmas gifts. Mr. Reinhardt at the time lived in a double log cabin with a wide entry between the cabins and only two fireplaces, one in each room below. The young ladies slept upstairs, where there was no fireplace, and they were told by Mrs. Reinhardt to undress in her room and go up to bed and the next morning slip back through this entry and come into her room and dress by the fire. In order to ascertain whether the young gentlemen were up, who slept in one of the rooms below, one of the girls came over their room (upstairs) and hollowed down, "Christmas gift!" They were answered in bed—that one could not be caught unless you could see them. Finding that the young men were in bed, the ladies came down and were all in Mrs. Reinhardt's room. The young men were informed of that fact, and one of them, who was quite playful, jumped out of bed, in his night clothes, and ran across the entry, opened the door of the room just a little, where the girls were, and hollowed "Chris"——, but before he could get the word out he was landed in the middle of the room by some unknown person. The girls gave a squall and fled in confusion—some under the bed, some behind Mrs. Reinhardt and the others no telling where. The young man rapdily retreated to his own room, without knowing by whom he was landed on the floor; but he always suspected Mr. Reinhardt. Mrs. Reinhordt came in and gave him a severe scolding for his rashness, and if he had not been her kin his acquaintance would have been cut and he would have spent no more Christmas eves there.

She was the mother of four children, only one of whom survives—Capt. Robert Perkins Reinhardt, the model farmer of Catawba.

There is also reprinted from the Morganton Herald the following, from the pen of the late Col. Thomas G. Walton of Morganton, which is interesting and historical, barring certain inaccuracies that will be pointed out:

THE PERKINS FAMILY
(Col. T. G. Walton in the Morganton Herald)

The Perkins family, of John's river, descended from a native of England, who came to the Colonies in 1732. Landing in Pennsylvania, he removed to Lincoln county, North Carolina (then Tryon), erected in 1779. By way of pre-eminence he was known as "Gentleman John Perkins." Accompanying an exploring party, led by a Moravian bishop (from Salem, now in Stokes county, erected 1789, the "United Brethren" having built a church there in 1763) before any grants had been issued by the State for the rich alluvial lands of John's river and Lower creek, which were then still untilled and unoccupied. Availing himself of this fact, he entered and obtained grants from the State for large bodies of the best land in Western North Carolina, devising the same to his four sons, Joseph, John, Alexander and Elisha, and daughter, Mary, whose offspring still own and live on them. The broad lowlands, having been cultivated in the various cereals for more than a century, without the use of fertilizers, show but little if any loss from the original productiveness. The name John's river was derived from "Gentleman John," perpetuating his name as long as flows the limpid water of this beautiful stream, from its source near the eastern base of the Grandfather mountain (said by distinguished geologists to be the oldest visible earthly formation as yet discovered). Joseph Perkins married Melissa Lavender, a relative and protegee of Col. Waightstill Avery, Sr. She was of French descent, probably Huguenot. (The name La Vender has possibly been anglicised from La Vendee, a meritime department in the west of France), by whom Joseph had three sons, Dr. James Hervey, Osborne and William, and four daughters, Elizabeth, who married Allen Connelly; Mary became the wife of David Corpening; Myra married Allen's brother, George Connelly; Mary became the wife of David Corpening, and Salena the wife of Levi Laxton. James Hervey and William died unmarried. John Perkins married Nancy Abernethy, who was a relative of the wife of Gen. Peter Forney of Lincoln county, a soldier of the Revolution. The maiden name of his wife was Nancy Abernethy, Mrs. Perkins being probably her namesake. Mr. Perkins died, leaving but one child, heiress to a large fortune in land and slaves. She married E. V. Michaux, a lawyer, who came to Burke in 1834 from Virginia. He was a relative of the distinguished North Carolinian, Nathaniel Macon.

Alexander Perkins married a Miss Moore (a relative of Dr. Bouchelle). By her he had three children, two sons, Theodore and Thaddeus, and daughter, Clarissa. The only surviving members of this branch of this branch of the Perkins family is Thaddeus, Jr., and his family, who are the sole owners of the splendid domain on Wilson's creek and John's river. Alexander and his brother John were the first to introduce horses of good pedigree in Burke county, breeding from celebrated stock in Virginia, belonging to William Amis and Col. Johnson. They took great pains in training them, and delighted in showing their superiority in fleetness and bottom at long distances on the Quaker Meadow and other race courses, over the scrubs of the country.

Elisha Perkins, the youngest son of "Gentleman John" (the ancestor of Alfred Perkins) inherited the fine alluvial lowlands on the west side of John's river, about three miles above its mouth, from his father. He died at an early age, leaving a widow and one son. The widow married Maj. Highland, who had distinguished himself during the war of the Revolution in battles fought against the British and Tories, and who was wounded at the battle of Ramsauer's Mill.

Alfred Perkins, a man highly esteemed for his probity, was a leading elder in the Presbyterian church. His death in the meridian of life was deeply regretted by all who knew him. He, like all the older members of the Perkins family, was of the bone and sinew of the land. He married Mary, the youngest daughter of Robert Caldwell, Sr., leaving at his death three children, Elisha Alexander, Robert C., and Elizabeth. Alexander reminds me very much of his father, in character, form and face,

"So near approach we their celestial kind
By justice, truth, and probity of mind."

"Parson Miller"

Mary, the daughter of John, Sr., married the Rev. Robert Miller, a native of England, a clergyman of the Episcopal church, a high-toned gentleman of the old school, dignified and blunt in manner (like most Englishmen I have known) yet benevolent and kind.

He joined in marriage the descendants of the old pioneers, and baptized their children, and prayed that God's blessing might rest upon them. He married my father in 1803. His dress at that time was knee breeches, black silk stockings, low shoes, with silver knee and shoe bucklets, with rubicund complexion and powdered hair. Thus, tout ensemble, he stood, prayer book in hand, a fine specimen of an English parson of Goldsmith's days:

"A man he was to all the country dear,
And passing rich with forty pounds a year."

He lived on a plantation left his wife, Mary, on Lower creek, his residence near the road side, named by him after his wife, "Mary's Grove." I remember his baptizing a child of one of Burke's leading citizens, more than sixty years since, who prided himself (as I think) in always redeeming his pledges. (In similar cases many, I fear, do not feel the responsibility resting upon them in becoming sponsors for children and taking upon themselves the solemn vows and promises required in baptism.) A large assemblage of persons were present, in what was then a part of the present building of the Presbyterian church. After the usual preliminary prayers, etc., preceding the promises to be made by the Godfather and mother, the question: "Dost thou, in the name of this child, renounce the devil and all his works, the vain pomp and glory of the world?" and so on to the end. To the astonishment of the congregation the response came from the father, loud and distinct, "I do not, sir." The parson looked at him sorrowfully in the face and said, "You will on the part of your child?" He replied, "I will on his part." "I wish you could say as much for yourself," said the parson. This is the only instance on record, so far as I know, where the matter had proceeded, as far as in this case, where the parent could not, conscientiously, and therefore would not, make a promise which he did not intend to fulfill—to his credit, be it said.

Alexander Perkins, the brother-in-law of Parson Miller, was a profane man, and frequently sorely tried the patience of the good man. Illustrating this, on one occasion he got the upper hand of the parson. He was on the way to market with a heavily-loaded wagon drawn by a team of spirited horses. The public road passed in front of and near the parson's residence, near the summit of a hill. The horses balked, refusing to pull. Perkins, irritated, beating the horses, cursing and swearing, brought the parson out, and, rebuking him for his profanity, he said:' "Brother Aleck, don't you see that all this abuse of the dumb brutes, and the taking of the name of your Maker in vain, does no good. Why, then, do you persist in doing so?" "Well," he said, "parson, that is so. I have tried cursing and beating them, with no effect. Now you get down on your knees and pray and let us see if that will make the horses pull the wagon up the hill." Leaving in disgust, he said, "Perkins, you are a depraved, incorrigible man." Mr. Miller left two sons and two daughters, one of whom, Margaret, married John S. Sudderth. The sons were Elisha P. and Nelson. The oldest, Elisha, married Sydney, the youngest daughter of Robert Caldwell, Sr. He was very popular, and was elected to the State Legislature from Burke in 1836-38, and from Caldwell in 1844-48.

PART I

JOHN PERKINS

Rev. Robert Johnstone Miller, son-in-law of John Perkins, made the following entry in an old Church of England Prayer Book, now in the possession of Mrs. Carter Beverly Harrison of Lenoir, N. C., great-great-granddaughter of Parson Miller:

"John Perkins, of Lincoln county, State of North Carolina, son of Elisha Perkins, of the State of Virginia, was born in Virginia, on the fifteenth day of September, 1733, A. D., and departed this mortal life on Friday morning at 5 minutes past 7 o'clock, the thirteenth day of April, 1804, aged 70 years and 7 months, wanting two days."

An old manuscript states that "John, the son of Elisha Perkins, was born the 15th Sept., 1733," but does not state where he was born. The same manuscript records also the birth of the children of John and Catherine Perkins, of the county of Rowan, parish of St. James, as follows:

(1) Elisha, born Oct. 18, 1760.
(2) Mary, born Oct. 6, 1762.
(3) Ephraim, born Nov. 6, 1764.
(4) John, born Feb. 11, 1767.
(5) Joseph, born Dec. 2, 1768.
(6) Burwell, born May 21, 1771, and died Jan. 20, 1773.

The above children were all born in South Carolina and Burwell was buried there.

(7) Alexander, born Dec. 6, 1773, at Island Ford, Rowan county, N. C.
(8) Sarah, born Jan. 8, 1776.
(9) Eli, born Dec. 27, 1777.
(10) Ann, born Dec. 27, 1780.

Burwell and Ann died in infancy. His wife, Catherine, was born Aug. 13, 1742, and died Oct. 5, 1819. The date of their marriage is not given.

It is interesting to note that there is internal evidence in the language of this old manuscript that shows it to have been written at an earlier period than the record of Parson Miller, which was made subsequent to April 13, 1804. At that date John Perkins' residence was in Lincoln county; at the date of the writing of the old manuscript the same place was in "the county of Rowan, Parish of St. James."

Judge McCorkle did not know where John Perkins was born. Col. Thomas G. Walton says he was descended from an Englishman who came to this country in 1732, landing in Pennsylvania and removing to Lincoln county.

Col Walton is probably correct, except as to the statement that Elisha Perkins came to North Carolina. He came no further South than Virginia when he left Pennsylvania, if he ever was in Pennsylvania. The part of Lincoln county in which John Perkins resided was, before the establishment of Lincoln county, in Rowan county.

I think it probable that Elisha Perkins, father of John Perkins, was one of the two representatives of Frederick county in the Virginia General Assembly that met at Williamsburg 1752-5, as contended by a writer in the Baltimore Sun of Dec. 8, 1907.

The first record of the appearance of John Perkins in North Carolina is found in the Colonial Records, wherein it is stated that the Moravian Bishop Spangenburg was introduced to him by Andrew Lambert, "a well-known Scotchman," in 1752. Earl Granville's agents had offered a large grant of the Earl's lands in North Carolina for a Moravian settlement to be brought from Bethlehem, Pennsylvania, and Bishop Spangenburg was leading an exploring and surveying expedition up the Catawba river in search of a suitable situation for his colony. At Island Ford he saw ahead of him, in his journey up the river, a very sparsely settled and untraveled country, infested with Indians, and felt the need of a guide. As such Andrew Lambert recommended to him John Perkins, a "hunter," and a trustworthy man. Bishop Spangenburg employed him and added: "I especially recommend John Perkins as a dilligent and trustworthy man and a friend of the brethren." At that time John Perkins was a youth, 19 years old, and had probably left the parental roof in Virginia within a year. To be accounted diligent and trustworthy is a fine character for a 19-year-old boy to have earned, and in this instance his history shows the boy to have been father to the man. This recommendation of the old Moravian Bishop will be more prized, perhaps, by John Perkins' descendants than the appellation of "Gentleman" John Perkins, which in after years was sometimes given to him. The grants he received for his lands from Earl Granville were all made to "John Perkins, Gentleman," following an old English form of grant, and that is the only reasonable explanation that can be given of the appellation of "Gentleman" John Perkins. A diligent and trustworthy boy, 19 years old and full of the spirit of adventure, would probably have started out from a Virginia home in 1752 on a prospecting tour armed with his trusty rifle and munitions and not heavily laden with coin, and would have found hunting through a region teeming with game of all kinds a comparatively easy means of livelihood, temporarily at least.

From Island Ford the expedition, under the guidance of John Perkins, set out up the Catawba river, and the Colonial Records describe their travels and set forth their surveys so minutely that the party can be trailed every step of the way. At the mouth of Middle creek or river (now John's river) the expedition left the Catawba river and traveled north up Middle river (John's river) from where it empties into the Catawba, near the present line between Burke and Caldwell counties, to its source, on top of the Blue Ridge, at Blowing Rock. The lands along this river are well described in the survey published in the Colonial Records that they are recognizable at this day. From Blowing Rock the expedition turned eastward and soon struck down the Yadkin river, which it followed till it arrived at what became its destination—Salem. The Moravians relinquished all right to any lands which they had tentatively surveyd.

Andrew Lambert, the "well-known Scotchman," did John Perkins a great service when he recommended him to Bishop Spangenburg, and it may be assumed that when the diligent and trustworthy lad, strong, adventurous and filled with high hopes for the future, set out upon his journey from his home in the Virginia valley, his highest anticipations did not foresee his prospects in any such measure as the future had in store for him. There is romance in life for all who strike out boldly, exercising initiative and individuality, provided there is also diligence and trustworthiness, and we are prone to believe that there is more room for the exercise of these up-building qualities in pioneer ages than in the days of complex civilization. It is true that the pioneer is a romantic character, but are not Edison, Bell, Morse, the Wrights pioneers?

Earl Granville's people were anxious to secure the Moravian colony, which was the most considerable settlement in one place they had been able to attract, and Bishop Spangenburg and his advisers were very influential with the land office. It is probable that John Perkins accompanied the expedition during the whole course of the journey, from Island Ford to Salem, and that he had been of much practical service to his employers. And it is not difficult to imagine that he had personal qualities of attraction that won the friendship of Bishop Spangenburg and his associates. It is not to be doubted that Bishop Spangenburg gave John Perkins all that he desired of the surveys, charts, etc., that were not to be utilized by the Moravians and that he exercised his powerful influence with the land office to make his young friend and erstwhile guide persona grata with the Earl of Granville's people. Else how can we account for John Perkins, a mere stripling, holding grants for thousands of acres of lands on John's river and having the river named for him? Col. Walton speaks of these grants being issued by the State, but there was no State then (as to those lands) and the grants came from Earl Granville. Such things have always gone by favor, and it is far from credible that John Perkins, the young hunter, however diligent and trustworthy and bright and resourceful he may have been, should have been able to ingratiate himself with the cold-blooded agents of the English Earl who were never known to give something for nothing.

Judge McCorkle tells of several thousand acres of land acquired in Rowan (Lincoln, and later Catawba), and Col. Walton tells of thousands acquired on John's river and elsewhere in Burke. He must have owned, on both the Catawba and John's rivers, between ten and fifteen thousand acres of the finest land in Western North Carolina. The Burke county lands were given by John Perkins to his children, Elisha, Joseph, John, Alexander and Mary (wife of Parson Miller), and his Catawba river lands, in Lincoln (now Catawba) to Ephraim, Eli and Sarah (wife of Thomas Snoddy of Surry). As Col. Walton says, all of the lands given to Elisha, John and Alexander belong to the family to this day, as does a portion of the lands left to Joseph and Mary Miller. To illustrate the approximate size of the plantations given to each child, it is to be noted that the share of John Perkins, Jr., on John's river, a beautiful farm of 1400 acres, a large proportion of it being broad river bottoms, descended to his only child, a daughter, in whose possession it remained until her death, in 1900,. Estimating the seven other shares of the estate of John Perkins, Sr., at 1400 acres each, we have 11,200 acres as the amount of his holdings.

Col. Walton speaks of Elisha Perkins as the youngest son of John Perkins, while he was really his oldest child, and Judge McCorkle does not mention him at all.

Judge McCorkle says of John Perkins that he was "every inch a man," and that "he had great pride of ancestry." He also speaks of the "Catherine Lowrance, the noble wife of John Perkins, who was an accomplished woman, well-bred." Bishop Spangenburg's estimate of him as being diligent and trustworthy at the age of of 19 years should be somewhat of an index to his character and a promise that there was the making of a man in him. He was very successful and became a wealthy man for that time and section, very early in life. In 1790, after he had settled his oldest son, Elisha, and his daughter, Mary, wife of Parson Miller, on fine plantations in Burke, he is credited in the census of that year with the possession of 13 slaves. At that period there were not as large holdings of slaves in the West as in the East; in fact, the West never did become as much of a slave-holding section as the East. Gen. William Lenoir, who had rich landed estates on the Yadkin in Wilkes, owned 12 slaves. Elisha Perkins owned 9 slaves in Burke and Mary Miller two in the same county, and it is probable that their father had furnished them with these negroes when he settled them on their plantations. So that, in that section at that time, the possession of wealth did not necessarily imply the ownership of vast "quarters" of slaves.

It has been suggested that John Perkins owed the favorable standing he was in with Earl Granville's land office to the friendly intervention of Bishop Spangenburg. Whether this is true or not, there is no doubt about his having been treated with the greatest favor by Earl Granville's agents, who necessarily exercised a powerful influence over the Governor and other servants of the Crown. As the troubles that culminated during the fateful days of 1775 and 1776 began to accumulate into a dark cloud rising over the country, we may be sure that they were the days that "tried men's souls." It was the same trial that a majority—at least a great many—of the men of the South went through when it came to the point of secession in 1861. It was not at all a one-sided question, proclaiming our independence of England. Of course we see it from an elevated point of view now and know that Mecklenburg and Philadelphia spoke the words of truth and soberness and that patriotism pointed away from the mother country; but there were then thousands of good, honest men who did not see it that way at all and felt that the world was turning upside down; that vested rights were to be done away with, and that radicalism, revolution and atheism were running rampant. It is a fancy that, until after the fight became hot, the word "revolution" was used as a term of reproach.

It is another fancy of mine that John Perkins, for one, took little stock in the insurrectionary doings in Alamance and could not understand why there should have been such high-talking, seditious meetings in Mecklenburg. He must have been of a like mind with thousands of other respectable North Carolinians, who just could not understand it all. What was all the bother about? The things complained of seemed trivial enough and they had no cause of complaint against the government that had been extremely good to them. Loyalty was a habit with them, a part of their religion, and they were rather dazed by the commotion. And it never occurred to them at all that there was any possibility of anything but trouble coming to many of their good friends who had gone crazy and were crying out against the King. They hoped, at the proper time, to be able to intercede and to lessen the blows that were sure to be aimed at many a hot-head.

Perhaps John Perkins did not think this way at all, but, recognizing that the ship of state was passing through rough waters, thought it the part of wisdom and prudence to sit tight, without rocking the boat, and tactfully to keep a cool head while so many other people were losing theirs by becoming wild partisans for or against the King.

A question of whether he was favorable to the cause of the colonies was raised in the committee of safety held at Salisbury at one meeting, and a committee was appointed to visit John Perkins for the purpose of securing from him a declaration of his principles touching the matters in controversy between said colonies and Great Britain. At a subsequent meeting of the committee of safety held at Salisbury the special committee reported that its members had called upon John Perkins in regard to the matters referred to them at a previous meeting and that the replies of John Perkins to the questions of the committee had been satisfactory.

The two paragraphs, above referred to, in the proceedings of the committee of safety, as published in Wheeler's History, always, whenever I have read them, inspired me with increased respect for John Perkins and are proof to me that he was a long-headed, broad-minded old colonial. He had no personal kick against the government; it had never occurred to him that there was any serious chance of the colonies becoming independent; but these people around Salisbury and Charlotte-town appeared to be in earnest and talked of self-government; he had no objection to majority rule and, as far as he could see into it, he was in sympathy with and would try to be further in sympathy with the people who were his neighbors; they said the masses were oppressed and, while he saw many abuses, he had not thought there were enough of them or such serious ones as to make it necessary to go to war about them; but, if the majority decided to go to war, he for one would not go to war against his neighbors. In other words, he could not stir himself into a passion over the course of the colonies, but he could assure his friends of the sub-committee that they might assure the committee of safety at Salisbury that he was not and never would be a—Tory. And that is about the size of the answer the committee took back to Salisbury from this wise old pioneer.

In 1883 the late Judge M. L. McCorkle of Catawba wrote a long contribution for the Newton Enterprise, covering the front page of four issues of that paper, which ostensibly was a description of the marriage of Ephraim Perkins, son of John Perkins, and Betsy Abernethy, daughter of David Abernethy, in 1800; the thread of the story was kept well, from start to finish, but the Judge ingeniously filled it in with the rich fund of information he possessed concerning all the best people of Lincoln and the neighboring counties. It is an extremely interesting collection of anecdotes, history, personal characteristics, and touching the Forneys, Brevards, Grahams, Abernethys, Hokes, Shipps, Millers, Lowrances, Lockes, McBees, Coulters, Shufords, Perkinses, Reinhardts, as a well as a delineation of manners and customs prevailing more than 100 years ago, and it deserves to be preserved more permanently than it is possible to be preserved for popular use in the files of an out-of-date newspaper. One of his most exciting stories is the account of the "infare" at John Perkins' house when his son Ephraim brought his bride home. After all the feasting and partaking of various other entertainments, the party closed with a horse-race and the company adjourned to the race course and witnessed a four-mile heat by four thoroughbred colts belonging to the master of the place.

It is probable that if John Perkins ever returned to his old home in Virginia after he came to North Carolina he must have done so subsequent to the Revolutionary war, for during the first years of his residence in this State he was busily engaged in building up his fortunes, and, by the time his estate and condition in life were such as to permit him to go upon his travels, the unsettled and distracted state of the country which continued up to and through the war, was not favorable for long journeys from home. It is presumable that, during the last twenty years of his life there was mutual visiting between him and his Virginia relatives, but at this day no letters or other documents are at hand to indicate it. Entries on the fly-leaves of an old copy of Shaw's "Justice" give the dates of the birth of his elder brother, Elisha, and of the latter's daughter, Elizabeth.

Besides, for thirteen or fourteen years John Perkins lived in South Carolina; for the old manuscript, after the record of the births of the first six of his children, adds: "The above children were born in South Carolina and Burwell is buried there." The eldest son, Elisha, was born on Oct. 18, 1760, and Burwell died Jan. 20, 1773. Alexander was born Dec. 6, 1773, near Island Ford, so that the return from South Carolina was between Jan. 20 and Dec. 6, 1773.

The late Judge A. C. Avery of Morganton wrote of John Perkins on pages 83 to 86, inclusive, in "Western North Carolina; Historical and Biographical; 1890, A. D. Smith & Co., Charlotte, N. C." Judge Avery says in part on pages 85 and 86:

"John Perkins, when he accompanied the Bishop, had an entry surveyed in his own name, including the Michaux place on John's river"—this survey covered practically all the land on John's river from the mouth of Wilson's creek, where it flows into John's river, a distance of perhaps ten or twelve miles, almost to the mouth of John's river as it enters the Catawba—"and afterwards, during the French war, in the year 1758, he took out a grant for it, being the oldest title to land in the county of Burke, as originally constituted. It is to be regretted that this patent was destroyed when the house of Mrs. Michaux was burned a few years since, and that the registry of it was also removed from the office and lost when Stoneman's raiders passed through this section in 1865. Perkins went over to South Carolina from his home at Island Ford probably in the early part of the French-Indian war, about 1754, and remained there for nineteen years. It appears from a copy of his family record, in possession of Capt. Alexander Perkins, that all of his children were born in South Carolina,

20

except Alexander" [and Sarah, Eli and Ann] "who was born near Island Ford, after his father's return in 1773, in a tent erected, we suppose, on the site of his cabin burnt by the Indians. John Perkins died three miles above Catawba Station. He had never lived on John's river, as most persons suppose, but evidently returned when the war was over to look after the land surveyed by the Bishop, and, finding that others had anticipated him as to that near the mouth of the river, he made entries in his own name from the Erwin place, then occupied by Sherrill, to the old Alexander Perkins place" [mouth of Wilson's creek]. "These entries include the magnificent farms occupied by his descendants, his sons Elisha, Joseph, John and Alexander having made their homes on them at an early day, while one of his daughters (Mary) married old "Parson Miller," who was the first Episcopal minister that sought a home in this country, and of whose Christian graces tradition has drawn a companion picture in simple prose to that of Goldsmith's village preacher." [The land given his daughter Mary was on Lower creek in what is now Caldwell county, and Parson Miller established himself there and named the place "Mary's Grove."] "He was the progenitor of the Miller family, most of whom now reside in Caldwell. The Perkins land on John river, except the Michaux place" [the share of John Perkins 2nd, who left one heir, a daughter, Susan, who married Richard Venable Michaux of Prince Edward county, Virginia] "like the tract near it" [20 miles away in Lincoln] "on the Catawba, was entered in Granville's office, surveyed by Griffith Rutherford, and again entered later in Burke county after it was established in 1777, surveyed again by Beekman and taken out of the office in 1780."

The unsettled conditions in the colonies, especially in the Southern colonies, during the French-Indian war, extending almost up to the Revolution, varied by temporary truces, treaties, etc., is matter of history and is graphically described on pages 155-160 of "Indians in North Carolina," Senate Document No. 677, 53rd Congress, 2nd session. In spite of truces, treaties, and a shameful, cowardly convention that Governor Dobbs appears to have entered into with some of the tribes, there was no real peace and there never could have been as long as the two races were keyed up to the highest tension by race antipathy and conflict of communal interests that gripped and held both sides eternally on the watch. And it was all perfectly natural—from the human standpoint. The Indians did not hate the white man except for what they considered the most real reasons. For generations they had heard about and some of them then living, upon occasional excursions down the Nickajock trail for hunting and trading, had seen with their own eyes, the whites firmly established in Albemarle and rapidly spreading out and growing westward towards the foothills. Now they saw them invading their own forests and hunting grounds, building cabins, appropriating their clearings, and making them larger by cutting down the trees. It was intolerable for an Indian to contemplate such a high-handed outrage. (Incidentally, it is interesting to note in this pamphlet, "Indians in North Carolina," the wonderful amount of booty the whites captured when they looted an Indian village—thousands of bushels of corn and thousands of pounds of pork and bacon; also to note the great number of slaves—prisoners taken in war—both whites and Indians possessed, all of Indian blood.) Ethically perhaps the whites had not so much logic for their position. But it was a condition and not a theory that confronted them; here they were, to settle and civilize a rich commonwealth, and all that stood in their way was a congeries of wild savage tribes obstructing them, like a dog in a manger, intent upon keeping the wilderness a wilderness and a desert for ever. And it is probable that the notion that no Indian ever becomes a good Indian until he dies was even a firmer conviction in the minds of the men of this age of flint and steel than it ever became in the minds of the men of the United States army during the seventh decade of the nineteenth century. I think it highly improbable that, under such circumstances as these existing, as high-spirited and adventurous a youth of John Perkins appears to have been would have turned tail and run away into South Carolina, and for this and other reasons I believe that Judge Avery erred in the supposition, which he did not strongly advance, that John Perkins went to South Carolina as early as 1754, only two years after he made the trip through the mountains with Bishop Spangenburg and not a great deal more than two years after his arrival in North Carolina. All his worldly, material interests bound him to North Carolina and it is almost certain that he never did leave Rowan county, Catawba and John's rivers until he was compelled to do so by circumstances that he could not overcome. I am satisfied he would have run the risk of danger from hostile savages. What he had to do, if he was a wise man, was to lead up from his surveys to grants from Earl Granville's land office. Work of this kind is not done in a day or a year, especially when ten or fifteen thousand acres of land are involved; it probably took him several years to perfect his titles. We see that, after he had gotten his grants through the Earl of Granville's office, the State took the matter up and issued grants after the war was over. This is true of the Michaux grant, so called—that is, that tract that afterwards fell to the share of John Perkins' granddaughter, the daughter of his son John. This grant issued in 1758, and I do not doubt that grants for the other tracts were issued earlier. The fact that the Michaux grant is the only one that was known to exist in our day is no evidence that the others did not exist, for if he had waited until after 1758 to enter the land surveyed by Bishop Spangenburg it is probable he would have been too late. If John Perkins ran away in 1754 he must have come back from time to time before 1758 to make his plats and to do all the other necessary and tedious things that lead up to the issuance of a land grant. He could not have ridden up to the Earl of Granville's land office and called out offhand for a grant for land, without "proving up."

I think that John Perkins did get into trouble, very serious trouble, that made it necessary for him to get away. I think that, in the course of his work of surveying, platting and traveling over the lands he was endeavoring to have granted to him, he had an altercation with an Indian and that he was forced to kill the red man. I believe the following letter of Governor

Dobbs, published in 5 Colonial Records 604, refers to John Perkins:

"Newbern, July 18, 1756.

"To Messrs. Waddell, Osborne and Alexander:

" . . . . I am sorry to find that there hath been one of the Catawbas killed by Perkins contrary to the express orders I had given to bear with ill usage and make a regular complaint in order to have satisfaction demanded of the Nation who is the aggressor and therefore if you have made up that to the satisfaction of the Catawbas and they wont be content to have him tryed and punished by the colony laws, I would advise you to give up the delinquent to them, as it is better that one should suffer who has done his utmost to bring on a National war than a whole community should suffer by his restiveness and disobedience and if he has made his escape do your utmost to apprehend him . . .   ARTHUR DOBBS."

The probabilities are that John Perkins left the State and went to South Carolina subsequent to the date of this letter. He was just 23 years old when this Indian was killed, and, if he killed him, I am sure he did it in self-defense. Now, that the Governor was guilty of the cruelty of trying to deliver him over (without giving him the rights inherent in every Englishman) to be tortured and burned at the stake, he realized that he was up against it and that it was the part of prudence to go away from the State.

John Perkins wife, Catherine Lowrance, was born Aug. 13, 1742, and when their first child, Elisha, was born, on Oct. 18, 1760, she was just a little more than 18 years old. Judge McCorkle speaks of her as the daughter of Isaac Lowrance of Bunker Hill, in Lincoln county, and that statement does not militate against the traditional statement in the family that she was born in the Union district, South Carolina, for it is plausible to conclude that, when John Perkins found it safe to return to Rowan county, his father-in-law decided to move at the same time to the new and rich country, where his son-in-law owned so much valuable property.

A pretty story touching Catherine Lowrance comes to me, through Mrs. Carter B. Harrison of Lenoir, a descendant of John and Catherine Perkins, from the late Miss Laura Norwood of Lenoir. Miss Norwood was a most charming woman, intellectual, cultivated, of brilliant wit and of great artistic talent which was highly developed and trained. Many women in North Carolina have learned from her at Saint Mary's and elsewhere the delicate and beautiful art of counterfeiting nature by drawing and by commingling, with pencil or brush, in harmonious combinations, the various tints of the rainbow. [Camouflage for "teaching art."] Miss Norwood had a taste for historical, biographical and genealogical research, especially about Western North Crolina subjects, and, being of Huguenot ancestry herself, took especial interest in Huguenot derivation generally. Knowing that John Perkins' son Joseph married a wife, Melissa Lavender, of Huguenot lineage, and that his granddaughter, Susan, daughter of his son John, was married to Richard Venable Michaux, a descendant of the old Huguenot emigre, Abraham Michaux, who established himself in Prince Edward county, Virginia, about the middle of the seventeenth century, she felt that it was according to the eternal fitness of things that Catherine Lowrance, coming from South Carolina, should be a Huguenot herself. Exactly upon what facts they founded their belief I do not know, but Miss Norwood and Mrs. Harrison fully persuaded themselves that John Perkins married Catherine Laurens of South Carolina. If he did he did not know it, for he spelled her name "Lowrance." It is to be admitted that John Perkins could not have qualified as an expert orthographist and that if he were living today he would probably be an advocate of the phonetic or simplified school of spelling, under the rules of which "Lowrance" might approximate the French pronunciation of "Laurens" provided the "broad a" were used in "Lowrance." In evidence that John Perkins antedated former President Roosevelt as a patron of simplified spelling it is only necessary to produce his family record wherein he spells the name of his son Burwell "Burrell," which he might have still further simplified as "Burl."

Judge McCorkle wrote around John Perkins and Ephraim Perkins' wedding to bring in the store of the personal recollections and traditions he possessed concerning the prominent people of old Lincoln, all for the entertainment of the readers of the Newton Enterprise; a detailed biographical sketch of John Perkins would have been "another story" for him and would have included much that was omitted in these interesting reminiscences. He was probably 55 or 60 years old in 1883 and, being connected by blood and marriage with the family of Catherine Lowrance and with the Abernethys and having been born and raised in the neighborhood where John Perkins had lived, probably knew about the latter's trouble with Indians and about his long sojourn in South Carolina. At any rate, the one episode is proved documentarily, while the other is almost certainly substantiated by documents and circumstantially. But fair dealing requires that Governor Dobbs be not convicted of endeavoring to deliver over John Perkins to the tender mercies and cruel practices of savage Indians unless it is proved. However, Governor Dobbs convicts himself of making the effort, in his timidity and panic, to bring that fate upon some free-born British subject and citizen of North Carolina, and no injustice is done him. From what we know of the characters of Messrs. Waddill, Osborne and Alexander it may safely be concluded that they practically ignored this ridiculous edict and that the most that they did in the premises was to warn John Perkins to keep as much in seclusion as possible while finishing up the work he had in hand in the matter of securing his land grants and then to disappear for a period until the clouds blew away. The probabilities are that he did not leave the State before 1758.

That the "clouds blew away" long before John Perkins moved back to Island Ford in 1773 is not to be doubted. He had left Rowan a young bachelor at least 15 years before that and when he came back to live temporarily in a tent at Island Ford, in which his seventh child was born in December, 1773, he was forty years old and brought with him his wife and five children. His long stay in South Carolina must have been caused by a certain amount of material prosperity and it is certain that he did

not come back empty-handed to the thousands of acres of land that had
been granted him by the Earl of Granville, every acre of which was part of
the unbroken forest when he resumed personal occupancy of it. This must
be so, for in 1790, seventeen years subsequent to his return, seven years
of which had been years of war and revolution, he was reported by the
first census, he and those of his children who were householders at that
time, to have owned 24 negroes. This indicates the possession of personal
and chattel property that should be estimated as considerable at the least.
The probability is that he brought most of these negroes with him from
South Carolina and that the first work upon which they were engaged was
clearing the bottom lands on the Catawba and John's rivers.

Living in a tent like Abraham of old, of course one of his earliest activities was to build houses and barns, and the first ones erected were doubtless
very primitive buildings. Later he built more pretentious houses. Recently I received two photographs from a lady who is a descendant of John
Perkins, one of which she said was the house in which John Perkins lived
and died on his Island Ford plantation, about three miles from Catawba
Station. The photograph is of a large, commodious two-story brick house,
in a good state of preservation, surrounded by fine old oak trees, which
indicate that there is, or had been, an extensive grove about the place.
There are brick chimneys at each end of the house and the entrance in the
center of the facade is covered by a small porch, although discolorations
on the upper walls show where there had been rafters to support a porch
or piazza running the whole length of the house, probably supported by
"colonial" pillars, as was the custom in the old days. The chimneys on
the ends of the house would make it appear that there was only one fireplace on each story and that one-half of the first story, at least, was one
big room or "hall," a style of building that was almost universal before
1800. The other phootgraph was of a tall mantel-piece, the shelf at the
top being suitable for the convenience of nobody who was not tall. It
appeared to be of cherry or walnut—some darkish wood, which could not
be identified in a photograph, and the carving was extremely pretty and
appropriate. The lady wrote as follows in transmitting the photographs:
"I am sending you some pictures of the old Perkins house at Island Ford.
Mrs. George Powell wrote me about the wonderful state of preservation of
the house. I have heard that the brick came from England. The old
mantel-piece is hand-carved and has a panel to match going around the
ceiling of the room. Then, isn't that old oak immense? . . . Mrs. Powell
also told me a story that had been related of Gentleman John—that he
had a race course on an island in the Catawba and that, after his fine
horses were groomed, he would rub a white silk handkerchief over them
to show if it would show soil, and if so the work would have to be done
over." I take the white handkerchief story with a grain of salt, as there
never was a horse raised that could be groomed so clean as that, and I
have never believed that the bringing over of so many brick from England
sounded reasonable. It is said that remains of the foundations of the grand-

stand and temporary stables are still to be seen on the Island. If John Perkins built this house it was of course done before 1804, the year of his death.

The years from 1773 to 1776 were busy years with John Perkins, who was deeply engrossed by his private business, looking after his farms and clearing and improving them, and paying little if any attention to public affairs and politics. But, never in the history of America, was politics hotter, more exciting or fiercer, and, if Pohn Perkins was not a politician, many of his neighbors were. Judge Avery used to tell, with great gusto, about a gentleman with political aspirations in the eastern part of North Carolina who was ambitious to go as a delegate to the national Democratic convention of 1896 and was canvassing some of his friends looking to his selection. One of these friends catechised him and put him through his paces as to his loyalty to the issue of the free and unlimited coinage of silver. He asked him question after question and at last irritated the candidate. "See here," said the aspirant, "there is not a stronger friend of silver than I am in North Carolina, but I am not going to be a damned fool about anything." "You won't do!" was the retort, and the gentleman did not go as a delegate to the convention. Some of John Perkins' neighbors had been watching him, listening to him and talking to him, and had come to the conclusion that his loyalty to the cause of the American colonies was just about on a par with what the Eastern North Carolina candidate's enhtusiasm for free silver was; so they reported him to the Committee of Safety at Salisbury, as the following extract from the minutes shows:

"Proceedings of the Committee of Safety in Rowan County, Salisbury, Sept. 20, 1775.—Resolved, that Captain Brevard cite John Perkins to appear before the next committee in Salisbury to give an account of his political sentiments relative to American Freedom.

"Oct. 17, 1775.—Pursuant to resolve of last committee John Perkins appeared. Resolved, that said John Perkins has given such account of his political sentiments relative to American freedom as is satisfactory.

"Resolved, that the principles upon which and the measures Christopher Beekman pursued in obtaining the appearance of John Perkins before this committee was reasonable and just."—See 10 Colonial Records, pages 253 and 280.

That last "Resolve," relative to the reasonableness and justice of Christopher Beekman's proceedings in "obtaining the appearance" of John Perkins, opens up a wide field for speculation. The committee gave John Perkins a clean bill of health politically, but he evidently wanted something more. He must have protested to the committee about the course pursued by Christopher Beekman in obtaining his appearance. I am inclined to believe that Christopher Beekman went to John Perkihs' house on the eve of the October meeting of the Committee of Safety and served the citation for his appearance; that John Perkins promised to be there, but that that did not satisfy Beekman, and that he arrested Perkins and, putting him under bodily restraint, took him as a prisoner to Salisbury. This is only surmise, but, if it is true, it was an outrage and John Perkins was right in protesting. However, in those hot times the Committee of Safety would have been afraid even to mildly chide so energetic a co-laborer as Christopher Beekman.

John Perkins' character as a patriot was established by the Committee of Safety's "Resolve" of Oct. 17, 1775, and was confirmed by the act of the General Assembly of 1777, which appointed William Sharp, John Harding and John Perkins, Esquires, commissioners to run the dividing lines between Rowan and Burke counties. 24 State Records, 29.

And it was further confirmed by the act of the General Assembly of October 23, 1778, which appointed John Perkins one of the thirty Justices of the Peace for Rowan county and a Justice of the "County Court and Sessions of the Peace." And Christopher Beekman was one of his colleagues!—23 State Records, 994.

From the date of his return to Rowan county John Perkins was in the midst of a busy career probably for twenty years. In 1790 he had given plantations to two of this children, Elisha, on John's river, and Mary, wife of Parson Miller, on Lower creek, when they married and "went to themselves," and it is presumable that at that time his affairs had so prospered that they did not require as close application from him as when he began the arduous task of clearing his thousands of acres of river bottoms. He started out well, with a good force of negroes; he was a man of energy, industry, foresight and expedients, and within the twenty years of his closest application to business, from 1773 to 1793, he was blessed with wonderful prosperity. Judge McCorkle pictures him as a country gentleman of affluence and there is no doubt of his having been a very wealthy countryman for that time and section. It would, however, not be a true estimate of his riches to measure them by the wealth of his four sons on John's river in Burke, for each of them was, when in his prime, a richer man than their father was in his day. This may sound paradoxical—assuming very properly that they did not add to their wealth of themselves—but it is due largely to the principle of the growth of wealth through the "unearned increment," as Henry George called it. The influx of population into North Carolina ran up the value of those four plantations on John's river so high that any one of them was worth more, when the master of it was 60 years old, than all of John Perkins' property was worth before he had given any of it away to his children. The principle will work out and is akin the one that water seeks its level; the higher the value of land the greater will be the net income from it.

The four "Perkins boys" received four magnificent plantations from their father on John's river. John's river heads in a cold spring near Blowing Rock and runs down through two valleys, the upper and the lower valley. The upper valley begins at the foot of the mountain and extends down about ten miles to Collettsville, the site of the old abandoned Indian village that Bishop Spangenburg notes as one of his camping places; the lower valley extends from Collettsville, 12 or 14 miles, to the mouth of the river, where it flows into the Catawba. John Perkins' grants did not extend out-side of the lower valley, three-fourths of which belonged to him. At Col-lettsville, and for some distance above, the hills extend down to the river on both sides and there is little or no bottom land, so that the upper valley has a generally oval shape and has always been called the "Globe," and, with some additions from surrounding mountain lands, is now Globe town-ship, in Caldwell county. In the latter half of the 18th century the Moores, Coffeys and Graggs moved in from Southwest Virginia, entered most of the land the bulk of it is still in possession of the descendants of the original entry-men.

Beginning with Elisha, the oldest, who received the Pleasant Valley farm, nearest the mouth of the river, the four farms extended up the river for six or eight miles to the mouth of Wilson's creek, below Collettsville, in the following order: Elisha, Joseph, John and Alexander, Alexander's farm being the furthest up the river from the mouth. These young Perkinses had been raised up with horses and when they went to Burke to live took with their horses their love for fine stock and a taste for the races, and it is very probable that they all had race-courses on their farms, unless an excep-tion be made of Pleasant Valley. Elisha died young and his son Alfred, only about ten years younger than his Uncle Alexander, became master at Pleasant Valley. As Alfred was a Presbyterian Elder there may be some doubt about his having had a race-course at Pleasant Valley. I have seen the remains of the track at Alexander's place and also the remains of the one at Mary's Grove on Lower creek at Elisha P. Miller's, a grandson of John Perkins. There were also very extensive orchards on these farms, the preponderating kind of fruit being a delicious, mellow summer apple called the "Perkins Red-graft," which John Perkins had introduced. It is an apple very like the Winesap and it is within the bounds of probability that brandy was made from the apples as well as cider. It may be that even Alfred made brandy. The Perkins apple goes by that name yet in Burke and Caldwell and is still a delicious fruit.

To indicate something of the value of these four Perkins farms on John's river the following interesting facts may be stated: Along in 1915 Thad-deus Perkins, grandson of Alexander and great-grandson of John Perkins, who owns the Alexander tract intact, gave an option on it for $80,000. It is true that the conditions of the option were not carried out, but the fact of the option gives an idea of the value placed upon it.

The tract of John Perkins, Jr., which lies just below that of Alexander, was held in undivided possession by his only child, Mrs. Richard V. Michaux, until her death in 1900. It was then divided into seven shares, all of which remain in possession of the heirs except two-thirds of one share, which was sold. This two-thirds of a one-seventh share of the John Perkins, Jr., tract was lately sold for $9,500. At the same rate the whole tract would sell for nearly $93,000.

The next farm down the river was the Joseph Perkins tract, which has been sold out of the family except a small portion of it. It was a magnificent farm.

The last tract, lying on the lower part of the river, is the Elisha Perkins tract, which has been held by many to have been the most valuable of the four, with the exception, perhaps, of the John Perkins, Jr., tract. One of four shares in this tract has been divided off and the three ladies who own the remaining three-fourths declare they would not take $80,000 for it.

ORIGIN OF COGNOMEN "GENTLEMAN"

I believe I have discovered the origin of the cognomen "Gentleman" as applied to John Perkins: It could possibly have arisen from the fact of there having lived in his neighborhood another John Perkins who was an uncouth, untidy, slouchy, "Slovenly Peter" sort of fellow and that to distinguish him from this John Perkins the John Perkins under consideration was called "Gentleman" John Perkins. But this is not likely, for there is no record or tradition of there ever having been another John Perkins, and, if there had been, such a neighborhood title would not probably have become so generally in use as it was in the case of John Perkins, or to have clung to his name for over 100 years after his death.

Of course if he had been a silly ass and had been in the habit of going about boasting and claiming to be a gentleman; for instance, because he was styled "John Perkins, Gentleman," in the grants made to him out of the Earl of Granville's land office, we can easily imagine that he could have secured for himself the title of "Gentleman John," bestowed in derision. But from what we have read of him and learned about him from tradition we have every reason to conclude that he was not such a fool as that.

The picture drawn of him by tradition is that of a man of good stature, well put up, of handsome appearance, "of commanding presence," and rather above the average physically. He was well-bred and well-mannered according to the times and the customs of the country in which he lived, and, in spite, perhaps, of an inclination toward a choleric temperament, manifested a due amount of suavity and consideration for other people. Men of that description are called gentlemen in these days, but no one thinks of selecting any particular one and dubbing him the gentleman par excellence because he may possess these admirable qualities. In John Perkins' days there were many other men in Rowan who possessed the same attributes of gentility that he did, and it is idle to suppose that the Scotch-Irish communiy singled him out for distinction as the model gentleman of the county, or of the Island Ford precinct.

It is a far cry from Salisbury to London, and it is safe to presume that the term "gentleman" as used in England was not synonymous with the same term as used in Rowan and Mecklenburg in those days. It is but a word, and yet these two uses of it, or rather the use and the non-use of it, are some of the indications that a line of demarcation was being drawn between the colonists and the loyalists that was to separate them into hostile camps in 1775 and 1776. The loyalists, who were back of the Governor and of the official caste, were the ruling class in the colony as long as the King's authority, as represented by his officials, was supreme. A revolt or a revolution is not the easiest thing in the world to foment among Anglo-Saxon people, and it cannot be accomplished unless a large proportion of the masses of the people jion in. A belief in the necessity for obedience is bred in the bone of this race, and those living in North Carolina in those days entertained, either from birth or descent, strong prejudices in favor of the mother country and it took something to overcome their loyalty to the King. In spite of their many follies, which eventually hastened their downfall, the ruling class, loyal to the crown, exercised many influences to control the masses and to hold them from going after the colonial agitators. These latter were probably the "intellectuals" of that day, young, educated, enthusiastic, inspired by the writings of the French "encyclo-pædists;" many of them well-born but hostile to the monarchy and favoring separation from England. It was their task to draw over the masses to their side, and they used all the means at hand, preaching the alluring principles of equality and liberty as set forth in the new philosophy. Their efforts met with great success in firing the popular imagination and was greatly assisted by the tactless policy of the royal government, which, as far as it was able, was as ruthless and careless of popular sensibilities as Louis the Fourteenth of France was when he said that it mattered little to him what happened after he was gone—even if the flood should come again! The climax was reached in May, 1775, when the action of the Mecklenburgers stirred the other counties, and, like a match set to shavings, started a fire that was never put out. The Committee of Safety of Rowan county was dominated by earnest, conscientious, fair-minded men whose solicitude was to control the enthusiasm of their followers without damping their ardor, and they desired to do strict justice.

When John Perkins was brought before the committee by Christopher Beekman, upon citation of Capt. Brevard, on Oct. 17, 1775, and gave a "satisfactory account of his political sentiments relative to American freedom," that was his vindication. But evidently John Perkins protested against "the measures pursued by Christopher Beekman in obtaining the appearance of John Perkins," or the committee would not have taken the trouble to pass a third resolve that these measures were "reasonable and just." It has been suggested that Beekman arrested Perkins and took him to Salisbury as a prisoner from his home at Island Ford. People are not always nice about such matters in war-times or in near-war-times, as we know from recent experiences. There have been instances of the arrest, in good faith, of perfectly loyal and patriotic American citizens upon charges of pro-Germanism, who have been, upon examination, released and exonerated. What would you do? To punish a citizen or an officer for arresting an alleged pro-German might tend to discourage the patriotic efforts of others and might result in injury to the country. One can write about it philosophically; John Perkins protested, and I am satisfied protested vehemently. I can reconstruct the scene: He denounced as an outrage his arrest upon a flimsy charge based upon no evidence, and his being brought to Salisbury as a prisoner, like a sheep-stealer, as if he were guilty of a felony—he, a true colonial and citizen of Rowan county, a gentleman and not a thief! It was a very natural protest and reasonable, but there is no accounting for the whims of a mob or crowd. The Committee of Safety was the people's supreme court and was always held with open doors. The mob was there and the term "gentleman" evidently used in the most unobjectionable sense, was taken up as being used in the loyalist sense, a sense that would have allowed of but a few gentlemen in Rowan county, none but great land-holders and justices of the peace. That was bound to be the sense in which John Perkins used it, for was he not brought before the committee on the charge of being unfriendly to American liberty? This was natural, too—natural but totally unjust. And so they echoed back at him—"Gentleman" John Perkins! They builded wiser than they knew, for though they dubbed him "Gentleman John" in reproach, the name spread and became general wherever he was known, and now, 115 years after his death, men call him "Gentleman" John Perkins, not in reproach and not knowing why, but supposing it to be complimentary rather than derogatory.

From the records it is learned that John Perkins never held any other office but that of Justice of the Peace and member of the Court of Pleas and Quarter Sessions for Lincoln county. Any library of books he owned must have been a miscellaneous collection, and, like all the colections of those days, would be very interesting to browse over in these days. I know of but one book he possessed, which I have—"Shaw's Justice," an ancient tome published in London in the middle of the eighteenth century, upon which were probably based his judgments delivered in his dusty-foot court of Justice of the Peace and from the bench of the High Court of Pleas and Quarter Sessions. It may be assumed that sometimes, perplexed by the complicated syllogisms of this old black-letter commentary, he said to himself in the words of Dogberry, "The law is a ass," and fell back upon his chimney corner digests and horse-sense pandects.

SOME OF JOHN PERKINS' MORE PROMINENT DESCENDANTS AND SUCCESSORS

His son, Ephraim Perkins, represented Lincoln in the Senate of 1805.

Ephraim's son-in-law, Franklin D. Rhinehart, represented Lincoln in the House of Commons of four General Assemblies, 1844, 1846, 1848 and 1850, and in the Senate in the General Assembly of 1858.

Two of Franklin D. Rhinehart's grandsons are Wallace A. Rhinehart, son of the late Robert Perkins Rhinehart of Newton, who is a member of the North Carolina State Senate, Legislature of 119; and young lawyer Murphy, son of Rev. J. L. Murphy of the Reformed church at Hickory. Both are prominent citizens of Catawba county.

John Perkins' son, Alexander, represented Burke in the Senate in the General Assemblies of 1815, 1817 and 1819. (Up to 1835 the General Assembly met annually; after that date biennially.)

James Harvey Perkins, son of Joseph and grandson of John, represented

Burke in the House of Commons in the General Assemblies of 1834, 1835 and 1836.

And Joseph Perkins' son-in-law, David Corpening, represented Burke in the House of Commons in the General Assembly of 1833.

Elisha Perkins Miller, son of Parson Miller and of his wife Mary, and grandson of John Perkins, represented Burke in the House of Commons in the General Assemblies of 1836, 1838 and 1840 and Caldwell in the House of Commons of the General Assemblies of 1846, 1848 and 1852, and he represented Burke and Caldwell in the Senate of 1858. He was the first Clerk of the Superior Court for the new county of Caldwell, 1840-1844. He was known as Maj. Miller of the old-time broom-stick militia, the officers of which were noted for their gorgeous uniforms, gold lace and ostrich feathers and the rank and file for their lack of uniforms and for their poor discipline; but he had a "war record" of 13 days, as witness the following declaration of Adjutant-General McCain under date of Aug. 3, 1916: "It is shown by the official records that Elisha P. Miller served as captain of Capt. Miller's company, 3rd North Carolina Militia, in the Cherokee war; that he was mustered in to date June 5, 1838, and that he was mustered out at Franklin, North Carolina, June 17, 1838." The Cherokee war was a bloodless conflict arising out of the removal of the eastern band of Cherokee Indians, under treaty, from their old reservation in the extreme western part of North Carolina to the new one in far-off Indian Territory. Some of them refused to go and assumed such a belligerent attitude that the authorities decided on a military "demonstration" and volunteers were raised and sent to Cherokee county. These companies were probably not technically cavalry, but they went on horseback. Two companies were sent from what is now Caldwell county—Capt. Miller's from the Burke section and Capt. Horton's from the Wilkes section. After 13 days of war's wild alarms these volunteers were disbanded in the Indian country, the controversy having been settled without bloodshed. As a matter of fact the Indians appear to have gained their point, for they are living there today on the eastern Cherokee reservation.

Dr. Alfred A. Kent (through Parson Miller), a prominent physician and capitalist of Lenoir, has represented Caldwell in the House; his uncle, A. Vannoy Miller, in the House, and his brother-in-law, Edward F. Wakefield, in the Senate. Dr. Kent and his son, Archibald, recently returned from the front in France, where he was with the 30th division, are both University men.

William C. Newland of Lenoir, through Joseph Perkins, has been a member of the House several times, as Lieutenant-Governor has presided over the Senate, and was a very able Solicitor of his judicial district for two terms. His nephew, Thomas Newland, a brilliant young lawyer, was also Solicitor of the district afterwards, and died in office, cut off upon the threshold of a promising career. W. C. Newland's father, the late Dr. Joseph C. Newland, represented Caldwell and McDowell in the Senate and House, and his uncle, Maj. Avery Connelly (through Joseph) represented

McDowell in both houses. Dr. Newland's wife was Laura, daughter of Allen and Elizabeth Connelly, Elizabeth being a daughter of Joseph Perkins.

Gov. Newland is one of the most popular of the public men in the State, and his wonderful geniality and the amiability of his disposition have won for him the affection and esteem of the people in his district as well as the confidence of the people of the whole State. Mr. Newland is a successful lawyer and began his career under bright auspices, being well equipped professionally, having a most popular turn for engaging the favorable attention of his constituents and being blessed by nature with a handsome person and pleasing address.

Capt. Nelson A. Miller, son of Elisha P. Miller and great-grandson of John Perkins, was captain of a Confederate cavalry company, was for many years on the Board of County Commissioners, was a successful and up-to-date farmer and was esteemed one of the most public-spirited of Caldwell's citizens. He was a popular man and was frequently pressed to become a candidate for political office, but he had no taste for politics and always declined.

William S. Miller, grandson of Parson Miller, a prominent business man in Lenoir, has been Sheriff of Caldwell, was long Postmaster of Lenoir, a position which son, W. Eugene Miller, filled for several years also.

Miss Mary Perkins was married to Horatio Miller Kent, descended from John Perkins through Parson Miller and his wife, Mary Perkins Miller.

Charles L. Schiefflin Corpening ("Shuff"), through Joseph, was the son of David Corpening and Mary, daughter of Joseph Perkins. David Corpening came of fine old Dutch stock, with the same tracings as the New York Schiefflins. "Shuff" Corpening, as he was universally called, was the successor to "Squire" Robert C. Pearson of Morganton as leader of the broadminded business men of the mid-western section of the State, west of Salisbury. Besides his wide business activities he was for many years Clerk of the Superior Court for McDowell county. His son, Charles M. Corpening, of McDowell, is a retired captain in the U. S. navy, having left the service during the Klondike excitement to establish and conduct an electrical plant for Dawson City. He is now living the life of a retired sailor on his farm. He goes back to John Perkins through John the second by his mother, Martha A. Michaux. His son, Max, recently graduated from West Point.

C. L. S. Corpening had four sisters, and his sister Laura married Leland Martin of Wilkes and they have a son, Philetus, who is a Judge of a Superior Court in a Texas judicial district. His sister Laura married Leland Martin's brother Philetus of Wilkes, and their son, Julius C. Martin, is a prominent and wealthy lawyer and capitalist in Asheville. His sister Julia married Joseph Lavender Laxton (whose mother, Selina, was a daughter of Joseph Perkins), a gallant Confederate soldier who came out of the war with only one leg and was for years a prominent Burke county physician and treasurer of the county until his death. Their sons, Ralph and Fred Laxton, are prominent in Charlotte as electrical engineers and business men generally. The fourth sister, Selina, married Col. Philetus Roberts, a brave Confederate officer who was killed at the battle of Bethel.

Joseph Perkins had two daughters, Myra and Elizabeth, who married two brothers, George Connelly of Caldwell and Allen Connelly of Burke. From Allen and Elizabeth Connelly are derived the Newlands of Caldwell, the Bergner Forneys of Burke and Maj. Avery Connelly of McDowell.

George and Myra Connelly had several sons and two daughters, and all of those surviving raised up families of children who have prospered and are among the best of the citizenship of North Carolina and of the country. Reference to the descendants of one of their children is made below:

Jane Connelly, great-granddaughter of John Perkins, was married to Sidney P. Dula, a well-to-do planter in Caldwell and for many years Clerk of the Court. On both the paternal and maternal sides Mr. Dula belonged to colonial families in Wilkes county who took prominent parts in the War of the Revolution. On the maternal side he was of the family of the eminent Presbyterian divine, Rev. Dr. John Witherspoon, president of Princeton College, who was a signer of the Declaration of Independence for the State of New Jersey. John and David Witherspoon of Wilkes were Revolutionary patriots, whose general service for the colonies and whose especially signal service at the battle of King's Mountain and elsewhere are graphically described in Draper's "Heroes of King's Mountain." Mr. Dula and his wife raised a large family of children, sons and daughters, and, soon after the civil war, moved to Missouri, where Mr. Dula went into the business of tobacco farming. Without going through all the details from the beginning of this venture until this time, it is sufficient to note its success: Caleb Connelly Dula, president of the Liggett & Myers Tobacco Company, and Robert B. Dula, a retired officer of the American Tobacco Company, both of New York and both great-great-grandsons of John Perkins, make the nearest approach to financial solvency of any of the old gentleman's living descendants, as they are accounted to be very wealthy, the pleasing epithet of "multimillionaire" being applied to them. Most of the members of this Dula family have shared in the wealth brought by tobacco, but Caleb and Robert are supposed to be the richest members of the family. "Bob" Dula, as he was called in Caldewll, was 17 years old in the last years of the war and when he arrived at that age went into the Confederate army, and, though he is not an old man, has to confess to being a Confederate "veteran." His father was in the army, as well as an older brother, George. His sister, Mrs. Laura D. English, of St. Louis, is much interested in everything connected with her great-great-grandfather, Gentleman John. It was she who furnished the photographs of his house.

Ward and Frank Powell are two rich young farmers living near Lenoir. Ward was County Commissioner a term of two, but resigned upon the plea that his official duties interfered with his private business. They are grandchildren of Sidney P. and Jane Connelly Dula, but have another line by which to reach John Perkins, being grandsons of Rev. John B. Powell, a fine old Baptist preacher, who married Margaret Sudderth, a granddaughter of Parson Miller and Mary Perkins Miller.

Jim and Ralph Connelly, bright boys who went through the University, are sons of Harvey Perkins Connelly, brother of Jane Dula, and the late James B. Connelly, Clerk of the Iredell Superior Court—(and don't they all seem to have had it in for the Superior Court clerkships?)—was a son of James Mortimer Connelly of Caldwell, brother of Jane Dula.

John Theodore Perkins, only child of Osmond and Mary Avery Perkins, is a Morganton lawyer and rated as being one of the ablest members of the Western North Carolina bar.

Dr. Walter Scott married Eliza, only daughter of Major Elisha P. and Sidney Caldwell Miller, granddaughter of Parson Miller and great-grand-daughter of John Perkins. Dr. Scott was for years before, during and after the civil war one of the prominent physicians of that section and was extremely popular, although he consistently declined political preferment. He was for eight years Treasurer of Caldwell county (1882-1890).

George Sumpter Powell, a prominent and prosperous Asheville capitalist, is a son of Nelson A. and Mary Sumpter Powell, a grandson of Thomas and Amelia Miller Sumpter, a great-grandson of Parson Miller and a great-great-grandson of John Perkins. George Powell's grandfather, Thomas Sumpter, was a nephew of Gen. Sumpter, the Revolutionary soldier.

Horatio Nelson Miller, a son of Parson Miller and grandson of John Perkins, was a farmer living near Lenoir and for a long time Clerk of Caldwell County Court. He was father of William S. and A. V. Miller and grandfather of the Kents.

Many more than half of the descendants of John Perkins live today beyond the confines of North Carolina and I have traced them to every State in the Union except the New England States. The above imperfect list includes such of his descendants (and, in a few instances, men who have married into the family) as, according to my fallible memory, have filled public positions or have risen above the average in business success. I do not doubt that I have omitted scores of names, in and out of the State, that should figure in that list as rightfully as those I have placed in it. In analyzing it it is interesting to note that not a single minister is found among John Perkns' descendants. Among them, scattered over North Carolina and outside of it, there may be and probably are some ministers, but if there are I do not know of them. There is a fair average of lawyers, newspaper men and doctors, and politics appears to have been of interest to each generation. But the great majority of the members of this family have taken naturally to commerce and agriculture. Up to the time of the civil war I do not find the members of this family to have been patrons of the University. Many of their women were educated at St. Mary's, Edgeworth (?), at Greensboro and Salem, but most of the pre-war boys appear to have concluded their studies at such schools as old Valle Crucis and Bingham's, and at those conducted by the very thorough old teachers of the class of Parson Miller and Robert Abernethy, at Lincolnton, "Classical Academy," and of John William Frederick Gates, Peter Stuart Ney, William Owen and William Lavender. John Perkins' son Alexander had a son, Theodore, who went through West Point, but I do not think he entered the army, as the army in those days was not big enough to accommodate with offices even the meager classes that graduated. The generation that was ready for college after the close of the war may be excused, for from 1868 the doors of the University were closed for several years. However, since the beginning of the new era in the life of the great institution the Perkins family has contributed its share of alumni.

The fly-leaf entries in the old Shaw's "Justice" are written in a bold, strong hand and were probably made by John Perkins himself; all the dates are put down as in "ye yare of ye Lord God," and there is no criticism to be made of the entries other than of the manner of spelling the word "year." But good spelling was not a universal accomplishment in those days and too much is not to be expected of John Perkins, who started out in the world when he was 19 years old. These entries are, moreover, some indication of how the word "year" was pronounced, if not by the generality, at least by the writer of the entries. "Ye yare of ye Lord God" is not Latin, but plain, simple, expressive, homespun English. The English translation of "Anno Domini" is "in the year of our Lord," and for two thousand years the bulk of Christians have read into the word "Dominus," and its equivalent "Lord" in English and its other equivalents in whatever languages they have used, the implication of the attributes of divinity; although the word has always been applied to human potentates and even to persons of lesser dignity. John Perkins was no controversialist, but his was the age of hot controversy and the ministers of all the churches preached a large proportion of their sermons in controversy with the teachers of infidelity and atheism who abounded in those days. Is it possible that he used a phrase that may have been for a time in use at that period to emphasize and to bring into prominence the belief in the fact of the divinity of the Second Person of the Godhead, which the atheists and infidels were logically bound to deny? It is interesting, because I never came across the phrase before.

When John Perkins first came from Virginia to Island Ford, a lad of 18 or 19 years of age in 1751-2, he was in all probability of Church of England proclivities; not that he needed necessarily to have been very religiously disposed, but because many Englishmen of that day, both in the mother country and in the colonies (especially if they had any connection with the colonial governments) felt that they owed a two-fold allegiance to the King—as head of the body-politic and as head of the Church. If John Perkins' father, Elisha, was the Perkins who, with his colleague, George William Fairfax, represented Frederick county, Virginia, in the House of Burgesses that met at Williamsburg from 1752 to 1755, he was a Church of England man and we may be sure that all of his family had been brought up as strict adherents of the State church. And Bishop Meade, in his "Old Churches and Old Families in Virginia," lists Isaac Perkins as a vestryman of the parish in which Winchester was situated, about the beginning of the Revolutionary war, showing that the Perkinses of Frederick were Church of England people. From the time when John Perkins came to

Island Ford until he moved to South Carolina, a period of six or eight years, there were no Methodists and perhaps few Baptists in Rowan and no other English-speaking Protestants except Presbyterians. While most of these Presbytrians traced themselves back to Ireland and their Irish Presbyterian Church owed its origin to the English Presbyterians, they were familiar with the fact of State Presbyterianism in Scotland, and probably shared the general indifference in Rowan to the whole matter of church precedence. The fires were smoldering, it is presumable, as early as 1752, but it was more than ten years before the agitation issuing in the battle of Alamance became acute. So the chances are that before he moved to South Carolina nothing occurred to interfere with John Perkins' youthful predilections, and when he returned to Island Ford in 1773 we may assume that his sentiments in regard to the Church at least were unchanged. We know that two years later doubts existed as to his sentiments in regard to matters of state, which he resolved satisfactorily.

Even if this were not known by family tradition to have been the case, there would be a strong presumption that his children, as long as they remained under the parental roof, were nominally if not by profession Episcopalians. Parson Miller, his son-in-law, was an Episcopal clergyman and Joseph Perkins, one of the sons, accompanied Parson Miller as a lay delegate from White Haven Episcopal parish to the Tarboro convention that elected Rev. Charles Pettigrew Bishop of the Diocese. But in the next generation the adherents of the Episcopal Church diminished greatly. John Perkins the Second had but one child, Susan, wife of Richard V. Michaux, and practically all of their descendants, with a few exceptions, are Episcopalians. The descendants of Mary, daughter of Joseph Perkins and wife of David Corpening, are the only descendants of Joseph Perkins who are Episcopalians. Even the family of Parson Miller was lax in its loyalty to the church of their father. The descendants of his son, Elisha P. Miller of Mary's Grove, are all Episcopalians, and so are some of the descendants of his son, Horatio Nelson,, and of his daughter, Amelia Sumpter. These are all of the Episcopalian descendants of John Perkins for whom I can vouch.

PART II.

ELISHA PERKINS, THIRD

Born Oct. 18, 1760. The maiden name of his wife is not known; after his death she married Maj. Highland, a Revolutionary soldier. He had a daughter, for there is a record of an Elisha Perkins Kincaid, a grandson; I know nothing further of them.

ALFRED was the only other child, who inherited the Pleasant Valley plantation. Col. Walton speaks of Elisha and his son Alfred. Alfred married Mary, daughter of Robert Caldwell of Burke, an Ulster Irishman who was "out in '98," and found it expedient to go upon his travels, winding up in Burke county. The daughter, Elizabeth, married a Mr. Williams and moved to Georgia, and Elisha Alexander and Robert Caldwell, truly par nobile fratrum, became owners of Pleasant Valley. It would take a book to record all the delightful things that could be written about these two brothers who owned everything in common as long as they both lived. Robert married Mary Neal of Hertford county, a niece of the late Dr. Richard Browning Baker of Bertie. She died within a few years. Later he married Emma Sue Gordon of Chowan. Alexander remained a bachelor for several years. He went into the civil war as captain of a cavalry company from Burke, Caldwell and McDowell. Soon after the close of the war he married Juliana Gordon, sister of Mrs. Robert C. Perkins. Mrs. Robert C. Perkins died childless; then followed the death of Mrs. Alexander Perkins, leaving four daughter for these two men to raise, and right well did they live up to their responsibilities. Alexander, the father, died first, leaving Robert head of the house, but the children had never known any difference between them. And then Robert died, but the four girls were then young ladies, and there, at Pleasant Valley, three of them live the ideal lives of country gentlewomen in their sweet home, the House of Hospitality, where the many kinfolks and hosts of other friends delight to congregate. Mrs. H. M. Kent of Caldwell, Mrs. Robert McConnaughey, Mrs. Robert L. Forney and Miss Sue Gordon Perkins of Pleasant Valley.

The late Justice Alfonso C. Avery of Burke, in his "History of the Presbyterian Churches of Quaker Meadows and Morganton," speaks as follows of Alfred Perkins and of his two sons, Elisha Alexander and Robert Caldwell Perkins:

"Elder Alfred Perkins

"Alfred Perkins was a son of Elisha Perkins and grandson of Gentleman John Perkins, who was among the earliest landowners in the fertile valley of John's River.

"Alfred Perkins was born —— (probably about 1785). He married Mary Caldwell, a daughter of Robin Caldwell and sister of John Caldwell, the father of Gov. Tod R. Caldwell. He was a quiet, unobtrusive gentleman, but by reason of his high character, sound judgment and store of general information he was naturally brought forward and looked to as a leader in church and state. We know that he was the Senator from the Burke district in 1817. His name was brought forward by John H. Wheeler as Senator 'A Perkins.'

"He was ordained elder during the pastorate of Rev. John Silliman. Owing to the loss of record of the session prior to 1835 the precise date of his ordination cannot be ascertained. But the minutes of Concord Presbytery show that he often attended Presbytery as a delegate during the pastorates of Rev. John Silliman and Rev. John S. McCutchan, and was an active and interested participant in the proceedings. It was he who expressed the assent of the church at Morganton to the dissolution of pastoral relations with Mr. Silliman and who obtained the sanction of that body to the call of his friend, Rev. J. S. McCutchan.

"Mr. Alfred Perkins left a daughter, Elizabeth, who married Mr. Williams and moved to Georgia; and two sons, Capt. E. A. Perkins and Mr. Robert C. Perkins. Like his friend and neighbor, W. W. Erwin, who lived on an adjacent farm, he left two sons who were elected elders in his old church and followed in his footsteps in leading exemplary lives.

"Elder Elisha Alexander Perkins

"Capt. E. A. Perkins was the elder of two sons of Alfred Perkins, the subject of a sketch already written. He was born Jan. 16, 1823, at his father's old home. Pleasant Valley,' on John's River, and died on Aug. 16, 1897. He was a quiet, sweet-tempered and modest man, but was unyielding in his adherence to principle and to what his conscience taught him was right.

"He volunteered as a private in the first company of cavalry raised in Burke county, which later was Company F of the Forty-first North Carolina, or Third Cavalry regiment; but on the reorganization of the company at the end of the year was elected captain and served in that capacity till the close of the. civil war. In his private life he was always deliberate, never known to be excited, and in battle was as cool and clear-headed as when engaged in his ordinary business in private life. He was distinguished for his uniform courage in battle. and his kindness and attention to his men in camp. Capt. Perkins was ordained an elder soon after uniting with the church in 1867, and as an officer of the church commanded the confidence and love of its members.

"He was married to Miss Juliana Gordon, a sister of the second wife of his brother, Robert C. Perkins, and of this marriage four daughters were born, all but one of whom retain their connection with the church and are among its staunch and liberal supporters.

"Elder Robert C. Perkins

"Robert Caldwell Perkins was born at 'Pleasant Valley,' on John's River, May 9, 1825, and died at his home Feb. 23, 1904. He was the only brother of Capt. E. A. Perkins.

"The two brothers lived with their mother until her death and afterwards occupied the same house until separated by death. The devotion of the two to each other seems to have been without parallel, even amongst brothers. They continued to cultivate a valuable farm, without a thought of dividing it or of a division of rents. They had but one purse and either felt at liberty to resort to it to meet personal expenses. At one time R. C. Perkins went, with a large party of North Carolinians, to California, where he spent some years in mining. But when he returned all that he had made in mining was mingled with the common fund arising from the profits of the farm under his brother's management. It was said that they never disagreed, though they consulted freely about the management of their property.

"Mr. R. C. Perkins was twice married, but no children were born to him of either union. He was first married to Miss Mary Neal of Halifax, sister of Maj. John B. Neal, who was prominent as a soldier and a politician. His second wife was Miss Emma Sue Gordon, a cousin of Miss Neal's, and whose sister afterwards became the wife of Capt. E. A. Perkins. R. C. Perkins seemed to love his brother's children as if they were his own, and lived with them until he provided for them before his death. He never sought public office, though upon the resignation of E. P. Moore as sheriff he was appointed to fill the unexpired term and proved a very efficient and acceptable officer.

"He had been installed as deacon before the death of his brother and was afterwards elected elder. He was upright and careful in the conduct of his business. He was firm in his adherence to principle and was esteemed as a model in his walk and conversation by the community in which he lived."

"Pleasant Valley Farm," on John's river, one of the richest and most valuable plantations in Burke county, is in acreage and extent just as it was when John Perkins gave it to his son, Elisha 3rd, something over 126 years ago, and undivided as to its broad acres, is the property in common of four ladies, great-great-granddaughters of John Perkins. Elisha Perkins left a widow and one son, Alfred, of whom Col. Walton says: "Alfred Perkins, a man highly esteemed for his probity, was a leading elder in the Presbyterian Church. His death in the meridian of life was deeply regretted by all who knew him. He, like the older members of the Perkins family, was of the bone and sinew of the land. He married Mary, the youngest daughter of Robert Caldwell, Sr., leaving at his death three children, Elisha Alexander, Robert Caldwell and Elizabeth. Alexander reminds me very much of his father, in character, form and face.

> "So near approach we their celestial kind
> By justice, truth and probity of mind."

Alexander and Robert bought the interest in "Pleasant Valley" of their sister, Elizabeth, who married a Mr. Williams of Mississippi. Robert married first Miss Mary Neal of Hertford county and, second, Miss Emma Susan Gordon of Chowan; he had no children by either wife. Alexander was like his father in being a Presbyterian elder. He was captain of a company of cavalry in the civil war. Somewhat late in life he married a sister of his brother's second wife, Miss Juliana Gordon, who was the mother of the four ladies who now own "Pleasant Valley"—Mrs. Mary Perkins Kent, Mrs. Emma Perkins McConnaughey and Miss Susan Gordon Perkins. These two brothers, from their babyhood to the death of Alexander, lived together and owned everything in common, and, at the death of Alexander, Robert entered into loco parentis to his brother's four daughters, who had never known any difference, in love and affection, between the two. Although Alexander was the older of this par nobile fratrum, as Judge McCorkle justly calls them for the sake of euphony, they were in common parlance always spoken of together as "Bob and Aleck" Perkins. The English rule of primogeniture would assign the headship of the House of Perkins in North Carolina to Mrs. Mary Perkins Kent, a charming and accomplished lady, a graduate of Peace Institute, who was married to Horatio Miller Kent, descended from John Perkins through Parson Miller and his wife, Mary Perkins Miller. The three other sisters, like their father and uncle, reside together in the fine old home at "Pleasant Valley," Mrs. Forney being a widow.

Robert Johnstone and Mary Perkins Miller

According to the records of the office of the Fourth Assistant Postmaster General at Washington, Lower Creek postoffice, Burke county, N. C., was established at Mary's Grove and Robert Johnstone Miller appointed postmaster, May 23, 1826, which position he held until his death in 1834. The postoffice was evidently created as a public convenience and not as a means of personal emolument for Parson Miller, who derived from the office in 1833 an income of $11.86. Perhaps he derived more benefit from the privilege the office conferred on him of franking his own correspondence, which was large. This was a privilege belonging to all postmasters, and in his case was all the more deserved because, as a Revolutionary veteran, he had consistently declined to apply for a pension, and so did his widow after his death. It is assumed that he availed himself of the franking privilege. Upon Parson Miller's death James Harper, Esq., was appointed postmaster of Lower Creek and moved the office a mile eastward to his large store at Fairfield, located just a mile west of where the court house in Lenoir now stands, and in 1841, when the town of Lenoir was established, the postoffice was removed to that town and James Harper made postmaster. So the present Lenoir postoffice may be said to be the lineal descendant of the Lower Creek postoffice established at Mary's Grove in 1826.

The Mary's Grove plantation, which was given by John Perkins to his daughter Mary when she married Parson Miller, was not a part of any grants made to him by Earl Granville, but was bought, either during or after the Revolutionary war, from Isaac Baldwin, a Tory, who deemed it expedient to leave the country. There was a "sprinkling" of Tories in the western section and one quite prominent lived but a few miles southwest of Mary's Grove, Col. Veezy Husband, a brother of Herman Husband, for whom was named Husband's creek in Caldwell, which runs through lands once owned by him. Lower Creek runs through Caldwell, past Lenoir, to the Catawba river, into which Lower creek, a Caldwell stream, Middle creek (John's river) running along the line between Caldwell and Burke, and Upper creek, in Burke—all three in Burke in those days—empty almost together near the line between the two counties. Parson Miller resided on the plantation from the date of his marriage in 1787 until 1792, during which period three of his children were born, moving back to Lincoln in 1792. In 1806 he returned to Mary's Grove, where he built the "hospitable mansion," where he lived until his death. The grove in which the house was situated was a magnificent collection of giant oaks and hickories; fifty years ago it covered a space of at least ten acres, and, though diminished in size now, is still a beautiful grove. During the first ten or fifteen years of his residence at Mary's Grove Parson Miller was away a great deal on missionary tours in North Carolina, Tennessee, South Carolina and Virginia, and his excellent wife was the head of the house and the manager of affairs.

In appearance Parson Miller is described as straight, dignified, above the average height, being a little under six feet tall, and of a benevolent but serious cast of countenance. He never gave up wearing "short-clothes"— knee pants and stockings—and his silver knee buckles and shoe buckles are in possession of a descendant now, in a very peculiar shape—that of silver spoons! The spoons are valued highly as relics, it is true, but they lack the personal sentiment that would attach to the buckles.

These were their children:

(A) John Wesley.

He was born at Mary's Grove, Dec. 23, 1787. There are no data at hand touching his history.

(B) George Osman.

Born July 8, 1789, at Mary's Grove; died March 18, 1805, in Lincoln county.

(C) Catherine Lowrance.

Born Nov. 15, 1790, at Mary's Grove. Married Rev. Godfrey Dreher, a Luthern minister in South Carolina, in which State they have numerous descendants of respectability.

(D) Margaret Bothier.

Born Aug. 5, 1792, at Poplar Hill, near Island Ford, Lincoln county. Married John Sudderth, a wealthy farmer on John's river. Their children were:

(1) Anne, who married Robert McCombs in Cherokee county, where numerous descendants reside, enjoying the respect of their neighbors.

(2) Sydney, who married a Miss Bristol of Burke, where their family still lives.

(3) John, who married a Miss Shuford of Catawba. A daughter married John S. Haigler, a great-grandson of Parson Miller.

(4) Margaret Bothier, who married Rev. John B. Powell, a much esteemed Baptist minister in Caldwell, who belonged to the family founded by an officer in Ferguson's army that was defeated by the colonists at King's Mountain. In spite of their having been on the royalist side in the Revolutionary war the Powells established themselves as a leading family in this section, and one of them, in this instance, married the daughter of a rebel veteran. Their children were:

(1) John M., who married Addie Dula; his history is set forth under the head of Joseph Perkins. Besides Ward and Frank, the sons, there are two daughters, Mrs. Jennings and Mrs. Throneburg.

(2) Horace, who married Miss Hartley. The husband is dead and the widow lives with her family in Virginia.

(E) Sarah Amelia.

Born July 23, 1784, at Poplar Hill, near Island Ford, and married, first, Col. Sumpter of South Carolina, a relative of Gen. Sumpter; married, second, Rev. Joseph Puett, a Methodist minister. The children were:

(1) Robert Sumpter, who went to Virginia at an early age; no data at hand.

(2) Caroline Sumpter, who married Albert E. Haigler of Lenoir. Their sons, Elisha P. and John S. Haigler, were gallant Confederate soldiers, who moved to Texas soon after the civil war and have become prosperous and prominent citizens. John S. Haigler married Miss Sudderth, a great-granddaughter of Parson Miller. Elisha married a Texas lady. Both have sons and daughters: Sarah, who married Capt. Stowe of Gaston county. They were married soon after Capt. Stowe came out of the civil war and moved to Kansas. Mrs. Stowe was a graduate of St. Mary's, Raleigh, and was one of the most accomplished women ever sent out from that great school. She left one daughter, Caroline Sumpter, who inherited her mother's beauty

and talents and also went to St. Mary's. Her well-trained and beautiful voice and her unusual gifts in the arts of drawing and painting early placed her among the foremost of the galaxy of remarkably gifted and talented women which the passing generation has given to Lenoir. She is married to Carter Beverly Harrison of Williamsburg, Va., a civil and railroad constructing engineer who later went into business and is one of the leading business men of Lenoir. They have a family of six interesting daughters. Mary, who married Samuel Hartley, one of the old-time business standbys of Lenoir. Both are dead, childless. Caroline and Amanda, twins. The former married, first, John L. Powell of Catawba, and second, Col. Gard of Florida. She is living in Lenoir, widowed and childless. Her twin sister, Amanda, married Lewis Brown of Salisbury, who later moved to Asheville, where they now live. Mrs. Gard and Mrs. Brown both graduated at St. Mary's, Raleigh.

(3) Mary Sumpter, who married Nelson A. Powell, a prominent manufacturer and farmer of Lenoir, and a brother of Rev. John B. Powell, above spoken of. Their children were George Sumpter Powell, one of the most prominent business men and financiers in the State, with headquarters at Asheville; and Lucy, who married her cousin, Tate Powell, of Catawba, and went to live in Mississippi and Florida.

(4) Elisha Perkins Puett, a Confederate soldier who died childless.

(5) Joseph Pinkney Puett, also a good Confederate soldier who survived the war many years. He married Miss Sally Haigler of Caldwell, and raised a family of worthy sons and daughters. He was widely known and respected in the county as one of its most sterling citizens: John, Joseph, Stella and Caroline.

(F) ELISHA PERKINS AND SIDNEY CALDWELL MILLER

Elisha Perkins Miller was born July 21, 1796, at Willow Hill, near Whitehaven church, Lincoln county. His wife, Sidney Caldwell, daughter of Robert Caldwell of Burke, was born at Londonderry, Ireland, in 1801, came to this country with her parents when she was six years old and died in 1875. She was educated at Salem Female Academy. Her sister Mary married Alfred Perkins and she was the aunt of Alexander and Robert Perkins, of former Gov. Tod R. Caldwell and of Robert Caldwell Pearson, at one time president of the Western North Carolina Railroad Company, all of Burke. An older brother, Robert Caldwell 2nd, was a wealthy merchant in Petersburg, Va., who, dying unmarried in 1818, left his fortune to his brother John and to his sisters. The considerable bequest left to Mrs. Miller by her brother's will enabled her to assist Major Miller to acquire the whole of the Mary's Grove property at the death of Parson Miller. Under the proprietorship of Major and Mrs. Miller Mary's Grove became and continued to be one of the notable seats of hospitality in Burke and Caldwell for many years. Major Miller represented Burke county in the biennial Legislatures of 1836, 1838 and 1840. The Legislature of 1840 created the county of Caldwell from portions of Burke and Wilkes counties and the county was founded in 1841. In 1842 Major Miller was elected the first Clerk of the Superior Court for the county. He did not exercise the functions of his office except by deputy, which was not a popular thing to do, and in 1844 he was defeated by a rising young physician, Dr. J. C. Newland. In 1842 and 1844 the county was represented in the lower house of the Legislature by William Dickson, a Whig friend of Major Miller. In 1846 and in 1848 Major Miller represented Caldwell in the lower house of the General Assembly. In 1850 his nephew, Tod R. Caldwell of Burke, was a candidate for the State Senate for the 46th district, and Major Miller supported his old friend, John Hayes of Caldwell, for the lower house, who was elected. In 1852 he was again elected to the lower house. In 1854 he was defeated for the Legislature by a margin of six votes by Gen. Cornelius Clarke, a Democrat. In 1856 he was again defeated by a small majority by Gen. S. F. Patterson, I believe. In 1858 he was elected to the State Senate for the 46th district. In 1860 his failing health took him out of politics and early in 1861 he died. For 25 years he was a man of great popularity in Burke and Caldwell counties and exerted a wide influence upon Whig politics in the western section of the State. Judge McCorkle calls him the "father of Caldwell county," a title which he perhaps deserves, for it is probable that, but for his exertions, the creation of the county would have been delayed several years. Elisha P. Miller had six sons and one daughter living at the beginning of the war; all the sons were in the Confederate army and were good soldiers:

(1) Robert Caldwell Miller was born in 1821 and died in 1873. As a very young man, in 1841-2-3, he was Deputy Clerk of the Superior Court of Caldwell county under his father, who was the first clerk. He was a fine business man and at one time was engaged in the manufacture of tobacco with Richard V. Michaux of Burke. When the collapse of the Episcopal school at Valle Crucis, in Watauga county (it was then Ashe county) came, Mr. Miller bought the property of the school, something like 2,000 acres, and turned it into a stock farm. He married Lucy Kendrick Abernethy, a ward and kinswoman of Bartlett Shipp of Lincoln, and had one son, Robert Caldwell. Both mother and son died within a few years. He was a member of Company F, 41st Regiment (cavalry) N. C. State troops, Capt. Perkins' company. Susan Fenimore Cooper, daughter of James Fenimore Cooper, in her "Memoir of William West Skiles; a Sketch of Missionary Life at Valle Crucis" (New York: James Pott & Co., publishers, 1890), which describes the missionary work of the Episcopal Church in Ashe county, after the failure of Valle Crucis as a school and mission station, makes the following reference to Mr. Miller:

"The property, heavily encumbered with debt, was sold, both land and stock, by the representatives of Dr. Ives to Mr. Robert Miller, the grandson of a Church clergyman of the olden time, who now worked the former mission ground as a farm. He was very kind to Mr. Skiles. The little office, or library, became the home of the missionary, who slept there, taking his meals, without charge, at Mr. Miller's. From the herd which had been so long his care the good Deacon reserved a favorite horse for missionary work, and several pet cows; and for these Mr. Miller also provided liberally. The missionary took all the care of the horse on himself. Henry, a fine, spirited roan, was already a sort of brother missionary, carrying his master faithfully, by night and day, over many a rugged path on errands of duty, or charity. The cows were reserved for the benefit of poor parishioners. . . . In the summer of 1853 a fellow-laborer in the good work came to assist Mr. Skiles, Mr. George N. Evans, a layman from Lenoir. He was received very kindly by Mr. Miller, who gave him two rooms in his own house, a front room with a fireplace and a bedroom adjoining, both comfortably furnished. A particular horse was placed at his disposal. For these conveniences and three bountiful meals daily the charge was three dollars a month! . . . Across the valley from the farmstead in the meadows beyond the little stream, labourers might be seen saving hay for a herd of fifty cattle. Near the buildings in the home field some twelve or fifteen sleek, straight-backed, small-tailed calves were seen gambolling and feeding. Night and morning a procession of twelve or fifteen sleek, glossy Durham cows came home to be milked. Of the milk and butter from this fine herd no account was taken; what was not eaten at table, or used for cooking, was left freely to the negroes. On the mountain was a large herd of fine Durhams, grazing at will. Every Saturday Mr. Miller went up to tne Alpine pasture to salt the herd; occasionally, for a holiday, Mr. Skiles and Mr. Evans went with him. After reaching the wild open pasture the usual call would be given, and in a moment the great creatures would come running, jumping, leaping, in their uncouth way, surrounding the visitors, their kindly faces and large dark eyes all turned towards their friend, the farmer. . . . It was a regular habit with Mr. Miller to take gun and hounds with him to the "salting." A deer was almost invariably roused on returning, and the crack of the rifle, with the baying of the hounds, was often heard from the pastures where the herd was feeding. The cattle heeded these sounds very little and were seldom alarmed by them, being familiar with the hounds. In one year, at this date, about 1854, seven deer were killed within the limits of Valle Crucis. . . . There were great fishermen, as well as hunters, in the valley. A brother of Mr. Miller was a very skillful angler. The finest of brook trout were on table almost every day during the season. Occasionally he would go to particular points on the mountain streams, familiar to him, equipped with rod and flies, and return in the evening with perhaps fifty or sixty trout, some of them nearly a foot long. Mr. Miller was something of a naturalist; rather too much so for the comfort of his friends. Among his pets was a live rattlesnake, a near neighbor of the missionary. He kept it in a cage on the porch. On one occasion when Mr. Skiles and Mr. Evans were passing through the porch after supper they heard Mr. Miller calling out in surprise: "Why, what are you doing here?" It was the rattlesnake with whom he was conversing. The creature was crawling about at leisure, having crept through the slats of his cage, flattening himself to an incredible degree to accomplish the feat. Mr. Miller, not at all discomposed, took the snake by the neck with a pair of tongs, and with the other hand held the tail, rattles and all, and coolly replaced it in the cage. On another occasion he was seen riding past the office with a bag of trout at his side, and over one shoulder a pole, with a live rattlesnake attached to it. He had seen the snake, caught it, tied it with a strip of bark to a tree until he had caught trout enough, and then fastened it to a pole, neck, body and tail, and, carrying the pole over one shoulder, rode quietly home with the deadly reptile at his back."

This idyllic experience of Mr. Miller, which, together with the other experiences of life at Valle Crucis, Miss Cooper describes so graphically and realistically as to raise her book almost to the dignity of a prose eclogue, occurred soon after his bereavement in the death of his wife and son, and no doubt the life he led here was more of a solace than any other occupation he could have engaged in. Subsequent to this came his business ventures, although he retained the Valle Crucis property for several years afterwards.

[It is interesting to note that Miss Susan Fenimore Cooper, the writer of the fascinating little book from which the above extracts were taken, was the daughter of James Fenimore Cooper, the great American novelist, was born at Scarsboro, N. J., in 1813, and during the last years of her father's life was his secretary and amanuensis. She died in Cooperstown, N. Y., Dec. 31, 1894, in her 81st year, just four years after the publication of her book about Valle Crucis.—From the People's Cyclopœdia.]

The Valle Crucis Estate

The following extract is made from Mr. Marshall DeLancey Haywood's "Bishops of North Carolina":

"It was in 1844-'45 that Bishop Ives began to take steps toward the establishment of a mountain mission in Watauga (Ashe) county at a place called Valle Crucis. This was a noble conception for the spread of religion and education throughout the mountainous section of the diocese, theretofore a much-neglected field; and, had he confined his religious views strictly to the teachings of the Holy Scriptures and Book of Common Prayer, the undertaking might have met with more success. Even with its early record, whereby it lost the confidence of the Church for a time, much good has been accomplished there. . . . In August, 1844, while on a visit to the Watauga Valley, the Bishop purchased a farm and awarded contracts for the erection of buildings for a missionary station. Of this farm, one hundred acres were under cultivation when the land was purchased. A small grist mill and tannery were already on the place. The first buildings erected under the auspices of Bishop Ives were a saw mill, a log kitchen and dining room, a log dwelling containing four rooms, and a frame building (sixty by twenty feet) with a room at each end for teachers, together with a large hall for school purposes in the center, all on the ground floor. Over the whole was a dormitory for boys. All these buildings, said the Bishop, would be ready by June, 1845. The objects of the Valle Crucis mission, as set forth by Bishop Ives to the convention of 1845, were as follows: To extend the gospel throughout a territory, thirty or forty miles in every direction, to a religiously destitute people; to give rudimentary instruction to poor children of the immediate neighborhood on terms which their parents could afford; to receive into the institution young men of talent from the surrounding country, on condition that they should serve as teachers and catechists for a certain time after graduation, under the direction of the authorities of the mission; to train boys of talent and merit for either the ministry or subordinate services to the Church; to give theological training to candidates for holy orders; to conduct a general school, both classical and agricultural; and to maintain a model farm, both as an aid in maintaining the mission and as a means of instructing the surrounding population in improved agriculture. This was the first school in North Carolina where practical agriculture was taught. The farm work was under the direction of a young agriculturist from the State of New York. In 1846 much progress was reported at Valle Crucis. Several of the old mills had been replaced with new and improved buildings for the same uses, and a large barn and blacksmith shop had been added, besides other houses. In the classical and agricultural school twenty-eight pupils had received instruction during the year, nine of these being given instruction and board free of charge. There were also seven candidates for holy orders residing there. Upon receipt of this report for 1847 the Committee on the State of the Church, through its chairman, the Reverend Robert Brent Drane of Wilmington, reported that it deeply sympathized with the Bishop in his wishes and agreed with him in the expectation of its ultimately becoming a noble and permanent nursery of the Church. In 1846 the Valle Crucis mission sustained a severe blow in the death of its first rector, the Reverend William Thurston. Of that faithful servant of God Bishop Ives wrote: 'As a friend, a presbyter, the rector of the school at Valle Crucis, and my associate in that self-sacrificing enterprise, his simplicity and guilelessness, and fidelity, and unflinching toil, had not only endeared him to my heart, but also made his loss a severe trial to my faith in the important work (to which I felt myself so urgently called) of spreading the light of life through our mountain wilds.' After the death of Mr. Thurston the Reverend Henry H. Prout became head of the mission and the Reverend Jarvis Buxton (son of the Reverend Jarvis Barry Buxton) had charge of the school. In time the Reverend William Glenny French succeeded Mr. Prout as head of the mission. In addition to those already mentioned in connection with Valle Crucis, quite a number of others lived there, at one time or another, who were either then in the sacred ministry or later took holy orders. Among these may be mentioned William R. Gries, William Passmore, George Patterson, Frederick Fitz-Gerald, Joseph W. Murphy, Richard Wainwright Barber, Charles T. Bland, William West Skiles and Thomas F. Davis, Jr. There were probably others also. In the report of the Committee on the State of the Church for 1848 we find the announcement: 'It is understood that the religious house at Valle Crucis will henceforth devote its energies to the instruction of candidates, or those who desire to become candidates, for holy orders. The importance of this institution to the diocese is immense, as the nursery of a future ministry. It appears to possess peculiar advantages for this work, not only in the retirement, for the time being, of its students from the distractions of society, and the hardy and useful discipline to which they are inured, but also in the great economy with which the work can be conducted—your committee being informed that $50 apiece, per annum, may be made to cover all necessary expenses, except clothing.' By 1849 the mission at Valle Crucis had begun to drift away from the teachings of the Church, and was fast becoming a feeble and undignified imitation of the monastic institutions of the Church of Rome. . . . In connection with the Valle Crucis mission it is but just to the clergymen there stationed by Bishop Ives to add that when he abandoned his Church a few years later not one followed his example. Their vow of 'obedience' did not carry them that far. After the defection of its founder the above mission was almost deserted for nearly half a century, though the Reverend William West Skiles faithfully labored as a missionary in that vicinity until his death, Dec. 8, 1862. The work there was revived, many years later, chiefly through the instrumentality of Bishop Cheshire; but it is at present situated within the missionary jurisdiction of Asheville, under Bishop Horner—an enthusiast on religious education—and is now daily doing the work for which it was originally founded."

The following has been written concerning Dr. Walter Scott, who was sent from Mr. William Bingham's great school at Hillsboro to Valle Crucis:

"He was sent to Valle Crucis, a school that had been established by Bishop Ives in the mountains of Ashe (now Watauga) county, about ten miles from Blowing Rock, at the foot of the Grandfather mountain. It was a 'grammar school,' with academic and collegiate pretensions, conducted in connection with a divinity school, and here were gathered the teachers of both schools, mostly ministers, as Dr. Thurston and Messrs. French, Gries, etc., and among the young divinity students, who also acted as tutors, was Dr. Scott's life-long friend, Rev. Dr. Jarvis Buxton, to whom he sent his son to school in after years, and who spent the last years of his useful life as rector of St. James' church, Lenoir, of which Dr. Scott was senior warden.

"The romance and the tragedy connected with the history of Valle Crucis are not a part of this story, but, in spite of the fact that the school did not survive the apostasy of Bishop Ives, during the few years of its existence it was a high-grade institution, and being situated in the highest, wildest, healthfulest and most beautiful part of the Blue Ridge mountains it was considered by many parents in middle and eastern North Carolina an ideal location for a school for their sons. Established in the midst of a royal domain of several thousand acres of forest, meadow and pasture land, rolling land for barley, buckwheat and other grains, Valle Crucis was a seat to arouse the enthusiasm of lovers of the chase, for all around it abounded deer and smaller game, and in the fastnesses of the Grandfather mountain quantities of black bear made their lair. Naturally the boys took to the sports and exercises that Nature afforded them, and, when the Christmas holidays came round, a lot of robust, healthy lads, brown as berries and almost as brawny as their mountain neighbors, returned to their lowland homes to illustrate the beauty of mens sana in cano corpore. Everybody had a gun of some kind, and Walter Scott, although lame, had the weak ankle of his shrunken left leg strongly braced and vied with the most athletic of his schoolfellows in field and woodland sports. He was a famous rifle shot and during his two years' stay at Valle Crucis brought down several deer. Once in a drive his stand was near the brink of High Falls and he heard the hounds in full cry coming down the creek; soon he saw a magnificent buck come loping toward him, and, lost in admiration of the beautiful apparition, he was overcome by 'buck fever' and forgot all about having a gun. Pushed by the hounds and terrified by the scent or sight of the boy lying in wait for him, the stag leaped frantically over the falls and down a precipice of ninety feet, to his death. These falls, near the Valle Crucis school, have a grandeur that would be sublime if the creek were larger, but it is only a large-sized brook or rivulet. On another occasion John Starke Ravenscroft Miller, a friend and schoolmate of Walter Scott and afterwards his brother-in-law, found a big buck snared, with horns tangled in a bramble bush, near the foot of these falls and boldly laid hold upon his horns, at the same time yelling for help. Despite the struggles of the deer he was held down until assistance came, when he was dispatched. That night there was venison for supper at Valle Crucis, a place was selected on the walls of the Hall for hanging a pair of antlers and the tanner was given a deer-hide to put in the vats."

As has been stated, Mr. Robert C. Miller eventually became owner of the Valle Crucis property and ran it as a stock farm. The Valle Crucis farm is referred to above as a "royal domain of several thousand acres." It was undoubtedly a fine piece of property, but that description probably is an exaggeration. An old manuscript memorandum kept by Mr. Miller in his Valle Crucis papers and dated 1845 sets forth the following items:

"Wm. Thurston and L. S. Ives; Deed from Joel Mast, 400 acres, recorded in Ashe.

"L. S. Ives to R. C. Miller, bond.

"1. L. S. Ives and Wm. Thurston, V. C. _____ 400 acres
"2. Entered in name of L. S. Ives _____ 100 "
"3. Entered in name of W. W. Skiles _____ 100 "
"4. Entered in name of C. & M., East Ashe _____ 50 "
"5. Hair Ridge, No. 11204 _____ 300 "
"6. Entry No. 11111, North of original purchase _____ 238 "
"7. Murphy _____ 25 "
                                                    _____
                                                    1313 acres"

Mr. Miller's 1313 included, it would seem, the "original purchase" of the "V. C." land, 400 acres, and 250 additional acres entered by the Valle Crucis people, not to speak of the 25 acres entered by Rev. Joel Murphy. He himself entered Entry No. 11111 of 238 acres. It is not clear by whom Entry No. 11204 of 300 acres was made.

(2) Eli Perkins Miller, born 1823, died unmarried in 1853, was a young man of marked business ability, handsome, a general favorite and gave promise of making a successful career for himself; he died at Asheboro, Randolph county, where he was engaged in gold-mining.

(3) Dr. William Walter Scott, born at Elm Grove, Perquimans county, married Eliza Snell Miller, the only daughter of Elisha P. and Sidney C. Miller. Dr. Scott was of old Albemarle Quaker stock, his father, William Copeland Scott, having lost his birthright by marrying Martha White "out of the meeting." He was a lineal descendant of that Joseph Scott, a mem-

ber of the Colonial Assembly, at whose house brother George Fax, the great English Quaker, makes record of sojourning during his visit to America in 1672, and where he held a "precious meeting," as stated in the Colonial Records. In the early forties of the last century William C. Scott, leaving his Elm Grove farm in Perquimans in charge of others, took up a temporary residence in Hillsboro for the education of his children, which move placed young Walter Scott under the tutelage of the distinguished educator, the late William Bingham, noted for the thoroughness of his teaching and the strictness of his discipline. From this great school he was translated to the Valle Crucis school and spent several years there advantageously. Whatever else may be said of Valle Crucis, it was a good school while it lasted. Major Miller of Mary's Grove had those of his sons, who were young enough, at school at Valle Crucis, and in the summer months resided with his family there much of the time. In this beautiful and romantic place Walter Scott met Eliza Miller and the result was that they were married in 1852. But before that event he had to finish school, read medicine with Dr. Richard Browning Baker of Hertford (later of Hickory), go to a medical college in Baltimore two years and wind up and graduate, as a full-fledged doctor, at Jefferson Medical College, Philadelphia. Then he was married and settled down as a country doctor at Hertford, Perquimans county. But Mrs. Scott, raised in the west, could not stand the eastern climate, and in 1854 he moved to Lenoir and began the practice of his profession there. Although lame from his childhood and exempt from military service, Dr. Scott was surgeon of Company B, 17th Battalion (Major Avery's command) and an examining surgeon for the conscript service, during the war. After the war he found himself, like so many others, high and dry financially, and in 1866 he accepted an offer to engage in the drug business in Norfolk, Va., where he remained until 1877, when, having somewhat recouped his war losses, he returned to Caldwell and settled on his farm, two and a half miles west of Lenoir, adjoining Mary's Grove; here he remained, practicing his profession and farming, till 1889, when he moved to Lenoir and engaged in the drug business again. He was Treasurer of Caldwell county from 1882 to 1890, the only elective office to which he ever aspired. His skill and success as a physician were well recognized in the State and the practice he was called upon to do was always greater than he could attend to, extending into the adjoining counties. As Mr. H. S. Blair, who wrote of him in the Lenoir Topic when he died, said: "He was beloved by all who knew him." No citizen of the county, however rich or poor, had any hesitation in sending for Dr. Scott, night or day, knowing that the question of pay would never come up till later and, when it did come up, that inability to pay would be as good as a receipt in full. He gave much to the poor and was beloved by the poor. His sweet and gentle character was well recognized by all who knew him. The old-time doctors were generally good men, and this is certainly true of Dr. Scott's old friends, colleagues and contemporaries, Dr. Scroggs and Dr. Beall; and we know that the Lord has given credit to these three worthies for much of free and loving service performed in behalf of the Lord's own poor, who are nearer to Him than the rich. Dr. Scott died Oct.

3, 1896, and Rev. Dr. Jarvis Buxton, rector of the Episcopal church in Lenoir, who performed the last sad rites, had been his preceptor at Valle Crucis, Dr. Buxton being a clerical student as well as a preceptor and Dr. Scott a lay student. He had been a member of the Episcopal Church from childhood and was Senior Warden of St. James' parish at his death. Mrs. Scott was educated at home, in Morganton, in Lincolnton and finally at Epworth School, Greensboro. The home school was under John William Frederick Gates (probably Goetz) whom Major Miller employed to teach his children; the children of neighbors also came to school to Mr. Gates and the children of Burke relatives came down and lived at Mary's Grove and enjoyed the privileges of learning under him. He was a German, tall, straight, military in his movements, strict in discipline at stated intervals subject to disappearing, upon which occasions he was generally credited (or debited) with being in his cups. Upon the rare occasions when he appeared openly under the influence of liquor he was apt to speak darkly of great European personages who were forced for political reasons to reside incognito upon foreign shores; he had probably heard the claim made by Peter Stuart Ney, the Iredell-Surrey school teacher contemporary with himself, that he was Marshal Ney in disguise. He was said to have been an excellent teacher, especially strong in mathematics. He was certainly a good "scribe." A well-bound manuscript prepared by Mrs. Scott is still extant, which contains on every page "examples" in the rule of three, tare and   and such intricate mathematical problems, worked out and written down in detail, and the writing is something marvelous. The most perfect mechanical "script" cannot excel it. There are some exquisite "copies" by Mr. Gates, which, however, do not much surpass in excellence the work of his young pupil. There are still living in Caldwell elderly gentlemen who recount with glee, at this late day, the powerful thrashings they received at the hands (and hickory switch) of "old man Gates." But this story is of Mrs. Scott. The rare character of this dear lady is a cherished remembrance to all who knew her. Duty, with all that it involved, was, to her, life; truth was everlasting, the opposite chaff. This creed, based upon her Christian faith, was the rock upon which she stood. The sweet simplicity of her nature invested her with a dignity that put her at ease under all circumstances; gentle but steadfast, never allowing tact to overstep the bounds of truth, there was something heroic in her mould; for the poverty of war times, the poverty of the times succeeding the war, the ungallant threats and abuses of invading enemies in arms—all were met with high courage and uncomplaining trust in a Power higher than worldly forces. In 1899, at the ripe age of 74, she passed away, but never during her life did she give the impression of being an old lady. Dr. and Mrs. Scott had four children, three of whom are living—William Walter, Jr., lawyer, for fifteen years editor of the Lenoir Topic and now employed in the Treasury Department, Washington, D. C.; married to his cousin, Mary Anderson Miller, who traces back to John Perkins both through R. J. and Mary Perkins Miller and John Perkins the second.—Robert Eli, died in infancy.—Martha White, married to Capt. Edmund Jones of Lenoir, N. C.—Mary Sidney Caldwell, wife of Rev. Dr. C. B. Bryan, rector of Grace Protestant

Episcopal church, Petersburg, Va.; seven children, six living: Elizabeth, wife of J. Morton Townsend, a Petersburg lawyer; one daughter and three sons living, one son died in infancy;—Delia, wife of George West Harrison, a Petersburg merchant; two daughters and one son;—Mary Sidney Caldwell, unmarried;—Corbin Braxton, 2nd, married to Alice Kent, one son; first lieutenant in National Army, booked for France but did not embark on account of armistice;—William Walter, unmarried, second lieutenant in National Army, booked for Siberia but did not embark on account of armistice. (Both C. B., Jr., and Walter enlisted, the one in the Richmond Howitzers and the other in the Richmond Blues, and received commissions after being detailed to officers' training comps.)—Frances Bland Tucker, unmarried.

(4) Nelson Alexander Miller was born in 1827 and died in 190—; married Adeline Wilfong of Catawba, a leading farmer, prominent in political and other county affairs, was for many years a member of the board of county commissioners, declined legislative and other official nominations which were often pressed upon him, was captain of Company B, 17th Battalion (Maj. Avery's command) during the civil war. His children: James E., a prospering lumbering and timber man in Louisiana; John W., a rich ranchman in Oklahoma, who has been sheriff of his county; Caldwell, prospecting in Montana; George Franklin and Robert Johnstone, 4th, are among the most progressive farmers in Caldwell; Lucy, an unmarried daughter, deceased; Eliza, widow of D. R. S. Frazier, a wealthy farmer and mineowner of the county; his mining property is in Montana and one of his farms is the rich plantation once owned by Col. George N. Folk, "Riverside," on the Yadkin. They have several fine sons who are making the most of the A. and E. College. John and Dan were in the National Army and John was in France during the great war. Steele Frazier was a genuine Tar Heel, but his father, old Donald Frazier, was a born Scotchman and set great store by the clan and plaid of the Highland Frasers. Scotch clannishness is proverbial. Old Robin Fleming, a Scotchman who died at a great age in Caldwell just after the civil war, used to come visiting down to Mary's Grove and, over his glass of toddy, would entertain Maj. Miller by extolling the glories of Parson Miller, of blessed memory, winding up with "The Scotch aye love ane anither." In old Burke—which included Caldwell—there must have been a good many Scotch, for Robert was generally called Robin.

(5) John Starke Ravenscroft Miller, born in 1831, killed at the battle of Winchester, Va., June 15, 1863. He was the fisherman brother of Robert Caldwell Miller, to whom Miss Cooper refers in her book, "Memoirs of W. W. Skiles." At that time he was young, in figure lithe, shapely and graceful, handsome and full of romance. We can picture him offering the fly to the elusive trout in the streams near Valle Crucis, with a volume of love sonnets near at hand. Love sonnets, since they were first indited, have been responsible for their share of masculine rash acts. A small matter, a little thing that most men would sigh over and soon forget, rankled in his bosom. He disappeared and it was perhaps a month or more before his family knew where he had gone. Then came a letter from out

of the West. He had enlisted as a regular in the United States army! This was about 1855 or 1856. He was in Albert Sidney Johnson's regiment, which was on its way to Salt Lake City to give the Mormons a lesson they deserved after the Mountain Meadows massacre. It was a long, tedious and dangerous expedition, but was well managed. After the Mormons had the curb placed upon them the regiment was sent on a campaign against the wild Indians up in what was then called the Nebraska country. This service was also long in duration and hazardous. By 1861, when the explosion at Fort Sumter took place, the young North Carolina soldier had become a sergeant-major of the regiment. Albert Sidney Johnson and the other commissioned officers had little trouble in having their resignations accepted, but it was more difficult to cancel an enlisted man's engagement. After considerable effort it was accomplished. Young Miller found himself a free man at Fort Laramie, situated in the northwestern wilds, the only inhabitants being wild and hostile Indians, and no roads leading away from it. To escape the almost certainty of death in traveling Indian trails he paddled in a canoe 1,000 miles down the Platte river, and, after many privations and much tribulation, reached Lenoir, N. C., in the course of a few months. He became adjutant of the 1st Regiment N. C. State troops. His military experience was extensive and practical and he was largely responsible for the fact that the First Regiment was soon recognized as a superbly-drilled body of men. Afterwards he was captain of Company H, from Martin county, in the same regiment. It is not proposed to follow him through his military career in the civil war. In 1862 in some engagement he was shot through the left foot just under the ankle, and this brought him home to Mary's Grove for a few weeks' furlough. This was the first opportunity his small nephews and nieces had had to become acquainted with "Uncle John," whom they had never seen before—except for a glimpse when he came back from the West and went right away again to the war— and whom they regarded as possessor of the all the spells of Romance. They hung upon every word of this engaging, debonair, knightly uncle, limping around on his crutches, who described to them with great gusto his adventures out upon the boundless plains, teeming with countless herds of buffalo, elk and wild horses and roving tribes of wild, war-like red Indians, with feathers in their hair, leather breeches and armed with dreadful tomahawks and scalping knives. They readily understood the emergency of his departure from this wonderful country and accepted his apology for not bringing them the Indian ponies, beaded moccasins and other wonderful gifts he had promised them in his letters to their parents. This war in which he was lamed was a prosaic, everyday affair, something they were used to and a necessary evil, for we had to fight the Yankees and would perhaps always be fighting them, but fighting on the plains with red Indians, stampeding herds of buffalo and droves of wild horses was altogether another matter and had romance in it, and "Uncle John," in telling of his adventures, was quite like a story book writer and the picturesqueness and romance of it all appealed to them. His wound healed and he returned to his post. A year rolled round and he returned to Mary's Grove—at least they were told he had returned, but they never saw him any more. What they did see was the little grandmother and their dear mothers weeping, a great crowd in Mary's Grove graveyard, the minister in his surplice having church and the filling up of a grave. From that day until they were nearly grown they never saw their mothers clad in anything but somber black, and the little grandmother's dress was black as long as she lived. Shot-through-the-head-on-the-field-of-battle. That is how it voiced itself to these children, and to this day this grim phrase associates itself with him whenever he is in their thoughts. Children, although they lose much of it when they grow up, have the dramatic instinct in a large degree, and immediately these little ones, in their imaginatons, saw ther gallant knight, after his exploits that were to them Homeric, ride out of the Elysian fields and mount a pedestal Tragedy had erected for him, and there he has stood ever since for them. For some time before Capt. Miller's death a vacancy in the colonelcy of his regiment was impending and soon after he was killed it actually occurred. He was almost the unanimous choice of the personnel of the regiment to fill the vacancy and it is probable that, if he had lived, he would have received the promotion. He died unmarried.

(6) Julius Sidney Miller, born 1833, died in 1862. Private in Company A, 22nd Regiment, N. C. State troops. He died in the service and was unmarried. A lovable, popular young soldier.

(7) Elisha Hamilton Miller, born in 1335 and died April 10, 1910. Private in Company F, 41st Regiment (cavalry), N. C. State troops. This lovable old bachelor had many friends and no enemies; his quaintness and small eccentricities but added to his attractions; he was reserved among strangers but, upon acquaintance, became affable; he was full of wise saws and queer and amusing illustrations; he knew all about woodcraft, birds, animals and fishes, and about the weather—if he bespoke rain it rained; if fair weather it was dry. He was a strict Episcopalian.

(8) Anderson Mitchell Miller, youngest child of Elisha P. and Sidney C. Miller, was born in 1837 and died in 1862. He was the sergeant of Company E, 6th Regiment, N. C. State troops. A handsome, tall, athletic youth, he enlisted at the beginning of the war and in less than two years died in the service; he was noted for personal bravery and is said to have laid himself open to benevolent reprimand from his superiors for recklessness in battle; a little experience, no doubt, taught him the expediency of not running too far ahead of the line of battle in a charge. In 1862 he married Mary Macon Michaux, daughter of Richard V. Michaux of Burke, and their daughter, Mary Anderson, is the wife of William Water Scott, 2nd.

(G) Robert Johnstone Miller, 2nd.

Fourth son of R. J. and Mary Miller, born June 1, 1798, at Willow Hill, Lincoln county. No data.

(H) William Sidney Miller.

Fifth son of R. J. and Mary Perkins, born March 18, 1801, at Willow Hill, Lincoln county. Moved to Georgia, where he married. No data as to his family.

(I) Eli Washington Miller.

Sixth son of Robert Johnstone and Mary Perkins Miller, born Nov. 26,

1802, at Willow Hill, Lincoln county. Died in 1820.

(J) Horatio Nelson Miller.

Seventh son of Robert Johnstone and Mary Perkins Miller, born ——, 180—, at Willow Hill, Lincoln county. If a man's name controlled his destiny "Squire Nelson" Miller would have entered the navy; he did not, however, but remained in civil life to become an honored and respected citizen of Burke and Caldwell counties, a Justice of the Peace, Clerk of the Court of Pleas and Quarter Sessions and a successful farmer. He married Caroline Vannoy of Wilkes, a noted beauty in her day, and raised a large family of pretty daughters and useful sons. Their children were·

(1) Col. Abram Sudderth and Mary Elizabeth Kent.

Col. Kent married Mary Elizabeth, eldest daughter of Horatio Nelson Miller, in the late fifties of the nineteenth century. He was the only son of a wealthy Virginian who came to North Carolina and acquired, partly by purchase and partly by marriage, extensive landed property on Lower creek, three miles west of Lenoir. The Colonel was rich, had much rich land, and could live in abundance without having recourse to the intensive methods of farming of the present day, which were not in vogue during his life. He loved stock, raised a great deal of it and consequently had extensive meadows. During th war he was a member of Company B, 17th Battalion (cavalry) Avery's command. A characteristic story is told of the Colonel by a young kinsman, upon whom he called just after the young man had returned from Raleigh bearing one of those wonderful "sheepskins" which the Supreme Court directs to be delivered, upon the payment of $20 in gold coin, to those ignoramuses whom they have examined and licensed to practice the profession of the law. The Colonel presented to the young man a carefully prepared list of data and directions and told him he wanted him to write his will. The youth was frightened and had not the nerve the most incipient lawyer is supposed to have. He flatly refused, advising his kinsman to seek more mature counsel; told him making a will was serious business and that, for his part, he did not propose to have generations yet unborn to rise up and call him cussed. "Fiddlesticks," replied the Colonel, "go and get help," and insisted so strongly that the young lawyer went to his old preceptor and, between them, they drew up, or, rather, the preceptor drew up, the will as directed, and he said it was a fine thing for the youngster, to whom the work and the experience were worth more than six months' hard study. When he took the will to Col. Kent and was asked to name his fee, he replied nothing: that the work and experience were enough pay. "Fiddlesticks," again retorted the Colonel. "Here are $100, which you will take and say nothing more about it." And the young lawyer took the largest fee he has ever received for writing a will. The old preceptor refused to share the we, but his grateful student made him take a part of it as a present. It is pleasant to record such generous acts on the part of the (then) young lawyer's very dear friends, Col. Abram S. Kent and Col. Clinton A. Cilley.—A fine old Perkins of the olden time was wont to say that "the Perkinses produce the finest women and the sorriest men of any family in the State!" Of course this was said in a manner of pleasantry, but more frequently in the presence of certain young Perkinses whom the old gentleman regarded as too "modern." These pages confirm the old gentleman's declaration that there have been many fine Perkins women. When some months ago it was published that Mrs. Mary Killer Kent was dead, aged 80 years, there was general surprise that she had lived so many years. Those who had known her long had known her first as young, beautiful and lovable, and she had kept that picture in their minds all through the years—a type of "Irish beauty," though she had not a drop of Irish blood in her veins, a beautiful blue-eyed brunette. Their children were: Horatio Miller (Horry) Kent, the oldest of the children, is a University of North Carolina man, a successful farmer and civil engineer and was a first lieutenant in the Spanish-American war. He married Miss Perkins, a great-great-granddaughter of John Perkins, through Elisha, and they have three children, Mrs. Julia Corpening, Robert Perkins Kent (married to Miss Anderson) and Mary Perkins Kent.—Dr. Alfred A. Kent, one of the eminent physicians of the State, prominent in all Lenoir activities, a leader in the Methodist church, one of the foremost manufacturers, a large landholder in the county and in the State of Oklahoma, all of which activities have made him a wealthy man. He has represented the county in the Legislature, where he introducd and passed many important bills of State-wide importance, a number of them involving hygienic and sanitary reform sand progress. His home, "Kentwood," located upon a commanding eminence, is one of the show places in Lenoir. He married Miss Anna Wright of Duplin county, and they have four sons and one daughter, including John A., a bright young fellow, just graduated from Chapel Hill (and late with the A. E. F. overseas), and Miss Olive, who prosecuted her studies at various seminaries in North and South Carolina.—Sarah, who married Edward F. Wakefield; she died several years ago, leaving two charming young daughters, Sarah and Lillian, the latter lately married to Mr. George Bernhardt.

(2) Elisha Perkins Miller, 2nd.

Upon the settlement of the estate of his uncle, Elisha P. Miller, Elisha P. Miller 2nd purchased the home section of the Mary's Grove estate and it is now in possession of his wife and children. Mary's Grove "God's Acre" —the graveyard—was reserved and is held in the name of W. W. Scott 2nd. Mr. Miller was a good Confederate soldier, serving through the whole war. He was a good citizen, a good manager of his excellent farm, and up to the time of his death took a laudable interest in the public affairs of the county. He married Miss Susan Hartley, a sister of Samuel Hartley, husband of Miss Mary Haigler, elsewhere spoken of, and left a large family of sons and daughters who are achieving success. One daughter, Nellie, married Logan E. Rabb, one of the most successful heads of the manufacturing interests of Lenoir. Little John Perkins Rabb is one of the few living namesakes of "Gentleman John."

(3) William Sidney Miller.

"Billy" Miller is a man of substance, engaged in a paying mercantile business in Lenoir, has been Sheriff of Caldwell county and postmaster of

Lenoir, and has raised a family of sons and daughters creditable to his family, among whom are: W. Eugene Miller, a popular young business man, who himself has been postmaster of Lenoir; Mrs. Edgar Allen Poe, Mrs. J. D. Matheson and Mrs. Elisha Harris. Mr. Miller married Miss Elizabeth Harshaw, of one of the leading families on John's river.

(4) Robert Johnstone Miller.

Robert Johnstone Miller, a grandson and namesake of Parson Miller, is the third of that name. He is an amiable bachelor who resides in Lenoir.

(5) John H. Miller.

"Jack" Miller was a "seventeen-year-old boy" in the Confederate service. Of this family only two of the sons went to the war because the others were not old enough. He was married twice, first to a Miss Young of Yancey county, by whom he had one son, who is a successful railroad man in California, and, second, to a Miss Tuttle of Mitchell, the mother of several children who survive their father, one of them being Alfred, in business in Lenoir.

(6) A. Vannoy Miller.

Mr. Miller is a farmer, is in business in Lenoir with his nephew, Alfred, has represented the district in the State Senate and married Miss Emma Harshaw of John's River; they have an interesting family of a son and two daughters.

(7) Laura Miller.

She is remembered as being, like her sisters, extremely pretty; graduated from St. Mary's, Raleigh; married a Mr. Dickson of Virginia and moved to Oregon. No details as to family.

(8) Eliza Miller.

The above paragraph applies to Miss Eliza Miller, with the modification that she married Mr. William W. Grant of Caldwell and moved to Virginia. A son, Wallace Grant, is known of by the writer as a creditable descendant.

(9) Alfred Miller.

A promising young man who died unmarried.

(3) Ephraim Perkins.

Judge McCorkle, writing of the marriage of Ephraim Perkins and Elizabeth Abernethy, says that they were married "about 1800." Ephraim Perkins was born Nov. 6, 1764, in South Carolina. Judge McCorkle thus describes them:

"Ephraim Perkins was about six feet high, complexion somewhat light, with blue eyes, fine chiseled nose, massive forehead and an intellectual countenance. . . . Betsy Abernethy was said to be the handsomest woman of her day. She was tall and handsome and her form and carriage were graceful and elegant. Her eyes were dark and sparkling and her hair as black as the raven's wing; her cheeks were as the sunny side of the luscious peach; her lips somewhat pouting, challenging kisses. It was said that the Abernethys received their dark complexion from their Pocahontas blood. Whether this was said in envy or as a compliment I cannot tell. The Scotch-Irish blood cannot be enriched by that of any people on earth, especially not by the Indian race . . . Her father, David Abernethy, lived in what is now Lincoln county, about six miles southwest of Beatty's Ford, on a plantation now (1883) owned by Miss Sally Lucky. The maiden name of her mother was Martha Turner. Her parents were from Virginia, but originally from Aberdeen, Scotland. She had six brothers, Robert, David, John, Turner, Moses and Miles, and two sisters, Nancy, who married Gen. Peter Forney, and Martha, who married Robert Abernethy."

From the above it does not appear possible for any Indian blood to have combined with Elizabeth Abernethy's Scotch-Irish blood. Judge McCorkle then goes on to describe the settling down to married life of the young married couple and to give some description of their children:

"Ephraim Perkins and his lovely bride spent their honeymoon visiting their friends. . . . After that they enter into a new life. They have to swarm out of the old hive . . . They were settled on a plantation not far from the home of their childhood, now owned by M. J. Cochran. In the process of time they became the happy recipients of ten childrens—five sons and five daughters. The sons were Elisha, who married Linney Sherrill, his neighbor, Enos Sherrill's, daughter; David and Daniel died unmarried; John married Elizabeth Norris and Robert married Elizabeth Martin, who died, and he maried her sister Matilda. The daughters were Adeline, who married Abel A. Shuford; Caroline married Colin Campbell of Tennessee; Catherine married John Beard; Elizabeth married Dr. Robert Adams and Martha, called Patsy, married the Hon. Frank D. Reinhardt, who represented old Lincoln from 1844 to 1850 in the North Carolina Legislature. Patsy was the youngest daughter. She was large, fine-looking, dignified and of excellent manners. She was full of kindness and benevolence. . . . She was baptized by her uncle, Rev. R. J. Miller, and afterwards, through his administration, confirmed a member of the Episcopal Church, the church of her father; but when she married she joined the church of her husband, the Reformed. She regarded the Anglican, Lutheran, German or Dutch Reformed and the Scotch Presbyterian churches essentially the same in their main features—justification by faith and salvation by grace."

(4) John Perkins, 2nd.

Judge McCorkle in describing the marriage of Ephraim Perkins and Elizabeth Abernethy in 1800 says:

"John Perkins, Jr., was there. For the first time he beheld Nancy Abernethy. She was not more than sweet sixteen, was well grown and had blue eyes, and was fair as the lily. The winds of heaven had never been permitted to blow upon her face too roughly. Her form was faultless, her movements graceful, her conversational powers unsurpassed for one of her age. Young as she was she sighed and felt no pain. John Perkins and she gave each other unutterable looks. They shortly afterwards were husband and wife and are the ancestors of Susan, consort of the late Richard V. Michaux of Burke."

Nancy was not there, for John Perkins, Jr., did not marry her until he was about 50 years old in 1816. From what has been handed down by tradition it is probable that all that Judge McCorkle says about this fair lady of the olden days is true, even as to her age when she was married, for it was a case of May and December mating. After the wedding John Perkins, Jr., took his bride home to "Old Oaks," the plantation on John's river given him by his father and namesake, which was the most valuable farm in Burke county. Three children were born to them but only one survived, Susan, who married Richard Venable Michaux of Prince Edward county, Virginia. Seldom is ever seen as handsome and distinguished looking a couple. She was tall, stately, shapely, beautiful, full of grace and dignity and yet withal gentle and sweet of disposition, and to her dying day, fifteen or twenty years ago, she looked the grande dame. Mr. Michaux was a proper consort for so lovely a bride. He was six feet and four inches tall, well-proportioned, easy of carriage and graceful. He belonged to to a Huguenot family that came to Virginia in the 17th century and had the blood of the Venables and Macons in his veins, being a near relative of our Nathaniel Macon. Mr. Michaux, although bred to the law and enjoying a lucrative practice, had a taste for agriculture and became one of the leading and most successful tobacco planters and manufacturers of the State in the days before the war. Mr. and Mrs. Michaux had three sons and five daughters, tall and handsome—the "tall Michaux": John Michaux joined the Confederate army at 17 years of age and died in the service. Richard Venable Michaux, Jr., was educated partly at Finley High School, Lenoir, partly at Hampden-Sydney, Virginia, and partly at West Point. He read law but never practiced. He is a bachelor and resides at the old home built by his father and called "Valley Farm," dividing his time between attention to his farm and devotion to his books. As his years accumulate he reminds his friends more and more of his distinguished-looking father in appearance. (Upon the death of John Perkins, Jr., his widow kept "Old Oaks" as part of her dower and Mr. Michaux built a modern residence across the river and called it "Valley Farm.")—William Macon Michaux, educated at Finley High School, Lenoir, is a farmer and lumberman, married Miss Carnelia Henderson and has a family of promising sons and daughters. Beautiful Mary Macon Michaux graduated from St. Mary's Hall, Burlington, N. J., the year the civil war began and married in 1862 Anderson Mitchell Miller of Caldwell, home from the war on furlough, who was a great-grandson of John Perkins through Parson Miller. He died within a year and his daughter, Mary Anderson Miller, is now the wife of William Walter Scott of Caldwell, great-grandson of John Perkins through Parson Miller.—Mrs. Mary Macon Michaux Miller was married, in second nuptials, to Moses N. Harshaw, a prominent lawyer, politician and farmer of Caldwell. Mr. Harshaw has represented his county in the Legislature, has been Solicitor, and is one of the most prominent of the Republican politicians in the State. Two sons were born of this marriage: (1) Jacob, deceased, who married Eliza P. Houck, daughter of John M. Houck; there was one daughter, Johnsie, the wife of H. C. Martin, Jr., who traces back to John Perkins through Joseph Perkins. (2) John M., who married Mary Houck, sister of Jacob's wife, and they have several children, among them Moses R. Harshaw, Jr., who ran away before he was 18 years old and enlisted in the regular army and joined the American forces in France during the great war.—Martha A. Michaux at the age of 16 married Chas. L.

Schiefflin Corpening, great-grandson of John Perkins through Joseph Perkins, who was for years Clerk of the Superior Court in McDowell county and a wealthy and influential man of affairs. They had three sons and two daughters: Richard Venable Corpening married Miss Anna Forney of Burke and died soon after arriving at his majority. Charles M. Corpening graduated from Annapolis, served for ten years in navy, resigning as lieutenant to go into business, and is now living on his farm in McDowell; he has a son, Max, who has graduated from West Point. Michaux Corpening is a successful physician practicing in Oregon. Two daughters, Susan and Patty, both married Connellys, of McDowell, and are residing, the former in California and the latter in McDowell. Katherine Michaux married David Laxton of Burke, a great-grandson of John Perkins through Joseph Perkins. Virginia Michaux, one of the most beautiful and popular women of Burke, died unmarried. She and her sister, Katherine, were graduates of St. Mary's, Raleigh. Bettie Venable Michaux, the youngest daughter, graduate of Kirkwood School, Lenoir, married Col. William S. Pearson of Morganton. They have a family of fine sons and daughters; their two sons are making good as business men.

(5) Joseph Perkins.

The family of Joseph Perkins was the most prolific of any derived from John Perkins and, next to it, the family of Parson Miller and his wife, Mary Perkins. Col. Walton says:

"Joseph Perkins married Melissa Lavender, a relative and protegee of Col. Waigghstill Avery, Sr. She was of French descent, probably Huguenot. (The name La'Vender has possible been Anglicized from La Vendee, a maritime province of France.) By her Joseph Perkins had three sons, Dr. Joseph Harvey, Osborne and William, and four daughters, Elizabeth, who married Allen Connelly of McDowell; Myra, who married his brother, George Connelly of Caldwell; Mary, who married David Corpening of Burke; Selina, who married Levi Laxton of Burke. James Harvey and William died unmarried."

John Perkins gave his son Joseph a splendid farm adjacent to and south of "Old Oaks" and "Valley Farm," but Joseph divided it up among his children and some of the divisions were sold out of the family, so that it is not easy to give the metes and bounds of the old place. The share of Osborne Perkins, who married Mary Avery, is intart and owned by his son, John T. Perkins of Morganton, an only child, who is one of the ablest lawyers in the State. (Mr. J. T. Perkins has sold his farm to Wallace Estes.) Harvey Perkins was sent to the North Carolina Legislature frequently from Burke.

Allen and Elizabeth Perkins Connelly.

Their children were:

Col. Avery Connelly, a wealthy and influential business man, farmer and politician in McDowell.

Laura Connelly, whose husband was Dr. Joseph C. Newland of Caldwell. Mrs. Newland, like her kinswoman, Mrs. Michaux, was noted for her many charms of mind and person and closed her earthly pilgrimage through a beautiful old age. Dr. Newland was a man of wealth and one of the prominent men in western North Carolina and had the management and control of large affairs in financial, mercantile and farming lines; as a young man he was Clerk of the Court of Caldwell and from time to time represented the county and the district in the House and Senate of the General Assembly. Their talented son, William Calhoun Newland, after graduating from Finley High School, Lenoir, had training at West Point and afterwards studied law with the beloved preceptor of so many North Carolina lawyers, Col. Clinton A. Cilley. Soon after coming to the bar he was elected Solicitor for his district, which, besides being a remunerative office, was a splendid school for grounding him in the knowledge of his profession. He is very popular and has, whenever he would permit it, been sent to represent the county in the General Assembly. He was elected Lieutenant-Governor of the State when Governor Kitchin was made Governor and the Senate has never had a more efficient presiding officer. Governor Newland is one of the most influential politicians in the west and the western people see a'long perspective to his political career. He married Miss Jessie Hendry, a charming lady, and they have an interesting family of three daughters and one son—Jessie, who is married to Rev. J. H. Day, formerly a Norfolk, Va., lawyer, who is now a prominent Baptist minister at Yonkers, N. Y.; Josephine, wife of Capt. H. H. Etheridge of the A. E. F. in France; Mary, married to Wilmar Mason Allen on Sept. 18, 1919; Mr. Allen is son of a prominent planter in Prince George county, Maryland, and will soon graduate as a physician from Johns Hopkins University; Benjamin, married to Miss Burleson of Mitchell.—The late Benjamin Newland, the genial railroad man who was for so many years a popular conductor on the Western North Carolina railroad, was a son of Dr. Newland, and by his first wife, a Miss Hallyburton of Salisbury, had two daughters, who married, the one A. H. Eller, a prominent lawyer and politician of Forsyth, and the other a Mr. Greene, a railroad man; and a son, the very able and popular Solicitor for the judicial district in which Caldwell is located, the late Thomas M. Newland, who married Miss Mary Wilcox, daughter of the late Dr. J. Orrin Wilcox of Ashe. Mr. Newland died while in office. —Another son of Dr. Newland is H. Theodore Newland—everybody calls him Fritz—one of the big business and financial men of Lenoir, who married Miss Bettie Tuttle of Richmond county.—And still another son was the late Augustus M. Newland, a successful lawyer in Newton, whose daughter married C. M. McCorkle, a prominent Newton attorney, son of the late Judge M. L. McCorkle, a connection and historian of the Perkins family.—John H. Newland was a son who died unmarried.—A daughter, Kate Newland, married Robert T. Claywell, a leading business man in Morganton; died in August, 1919.—The youngest daughter, Alma Newland, was the first wife of Jacob C. Seale, a prominent business man of Lenoir; she left a sweet young daughter, Alma Newland Seagle.

Mary Perkins married Bergner Forney, a wealthy Burke county farmer. They had one son, John Perkins Forney, who died unmarried, and six beautiful and accomplished daughters, two of whom died unmarried and the remaining four of whom ma.ried respectively Pleasant G. Moore, one of the leading citizens of Caldwell, at the head of large manufacturing interests; John Bohannon and Edward Shut .d of Hickory, Catawba county, of which city they were leading citizen .nd business men, and Samuel McDowell, a Burke county farmer and b .iness man.

George and Myra Perkins Connel. .

George Connelly was a brother of Allen Connelly, and Judge McCorkle thus refers to him and his wife: "Myra was tne elegant and accomplished daughter of Joseph and Melissa _ .ender Perkins, who married George Connelly, late oı Caldwell county; they were the parents of Mortimer Connelly, Esq., of Caldwell, and grandparents of Judge James Connelly of Iredell." They had two daughters noted for their remaikable beauty, Adelaide and Jane, and four sons, Momtimer, Larvey Perkins, Julius and Caleb Adelaide Connelly married Major Robe.. B. Bogle of Caldwell and had two children, William Gaither and Ade...de, both of whom inherited their mother's great beauty, the son having been accounted one of the handsomest men and the daughter one of the most beautnul women of their day in that section. William G. Bogle died childless. Adelaide married Dr. Little of Watauga, where they now reside, surrounded by a family of interesting sons and daughters.

Jane Connelly married Sidney P. Dula, at one time a wealthy and at all times a popular and influential citizen of Caldwell and member of a leading families in the county. For years he was Clerk of the old Court of Pleas and Quarter Sessions. As in the case of so many other Southern citizens, his fortunes were shattered by the civil war, at the close of which settled in Anson county) and settled in Missouri, where he entered upon ily (with the exception of his eldest son, George Dula, who married and settled in Anson county) and settled in Missouri, whree he entered upon the business of tobacco planting. George Dula, the oldest son, was in the military service as a "seventeen-year-old boy," and his brother, Robert B., though much too young for such work, would upon frequent occasions toward the close of the war, "jine the cavalry," which was kept busy repelling raids upon the county from East Tennessee. The first years in Missouri were naturally difficult, but as years went by and as the three sons who went with their father grew up, the crops of tobacco began to pay, they went into the manufacture of the weed and, to make a long story short, Robert B. Dula and Caleb Connelly Dula are now living in New York city, at the head of great tobacco interests, millionaires "many times over," the richest men who were ever citizens of Caldwell county.—Their brother Adolphus died several years ago.—From the information at hand there were three sisters: Mrs. English, who married in St. Louis, and who shared in the prosperity brought about by the tobacco industry; Ella, who married Lucius Corpening of Burke, and whose prospects were evidently not injured by the prosperity of her family; and Addie, who married John Miller Powell, a great-great-grandson of John Perkins through Parson Miller. John Powell was one of the best farmers in Caldwell and made money in the days when farming was not considered a money-making profession. His two sons, Ward and Frank, followed in his footsteps and are not only getting rich but are rated as rich men. Ward was County Commissioner for two years but refused a renomination; he could not afford it! Ward is a bachelor; Frank married a Miss Greer.

J. Mortimer Connelly, a most lovable man, married Miss Emily Parks of Wilkes. Everybody recognized the gentleness and kind-heartedness of this worthy couple. Besides James B. Connelly, who was Clerk of the Superior Court of Iredell county for many years, there are these sons: Oliver, Walter, John and George, and two daughters who married gentlemen by the name of Gentry in Alleghany, and one unmarried daughter.

Harvey Perkins Connelly married Josephine Dula, niece of Sidney P. Dula, and left a large family of sons and daughters. George Wallace Connelly is a prosperous business man in Indiana. Ralph is electrical engineer for the municipality of Charlotte, and James is principal of a graded school in an eastern city.

Julius and Caleb Connelly died unmarried.

David and Mary Perkins Corpening.

David Corpening, who married Joseph Perkins' daughter Mary, was a wealthy Burke county farmer of Dutch descent. They had the following children:

Charles L. Schiefflin Corpening, who married Martha A. Michaux, granddaughter of (4) John Perkins, 2nd. under which head his history is set forth.

Thomas Corpening, who settled in Statesville, Iredell county, where for many years he was a successful dentist. One of his daughters was the second wife of the late Judge Furches.

Julius Corpening, who married and settled in Buncombe county.

Laura Corpening, who married the late Lee Martin of Wilkes. Harry C. Martin, newspaper man and business man of Lenoir, and Judge Philetus Martin of Texas are their sons.

Virginia Corpening married Philetus Martin of Wilkes. Julius C. Martin, a prominent Asheville lawyer, is their son.

Julia Corpening married Joseph Lavender Laxton, grandson of Joseph Perkins, a gallant Confederate officer who lost a leg in the war, and one of the foremost physicians in Morganton at the time of his death.

Selina Corpening married Col. Philetus Roberts of Asheville. Mrs. Roberts was a gentlewoman in very truth, and her sweet and engaging disposition made her a general favorite. Their children were Thomas, Laura, Lucy, Catherine and Bettie (Bethel). All except Laura and Bethel died unmarried. Laura married Norman Girdwood, a wealthy Scotchman of Asheville, and has since died. Bethel, who was so named because she was born on the day of the battle of Bethel, in which Col. Roberts was killed, married Ephraim Clayton, an Asheville business man, and is living.

Celia Corpening married Dr. James Stephens of Leicester, Buncombe county, and their family is one of prominence in the county.

Levi and Selina Perkins Laxton.

Their son, Dr. Joseph Lavender Laxton, and his wife, Julia Corpening, have been spoken of under the head of David and Mary Corpening. They have two sons, Robert and Frederick, prominent business men in Charlotte, and several talented daughters. Fred married Miss Annie Erwin, daughter of the late Col. George Phifer Erwin of Morganton, and Ralph married Miss Knabe of Knoxville, Tenn.

Romulus Laxton, living on John's river, was, like his brother Lavender, a brave Confederate soldier; he was married first to Miss Parks of Wilkes, and, second, to Miss Tate of Burke, and has a large family of sons and daughters, who, keeping in step with the "New South," are making the most of their lives and prospering.

David Laxton married Miss Kate Michaux, spoken of under the head of (4) John Perkins, 2nd. Both are dead and have two children possessing shares of the estates left by (4) John Perkins, 2nd, and by (5) Joseph Perkins—Charles and Lucy Laxton, respected citizens of Burke.

(7) Alexander Perkins.

Alexander Perkins married Rebecca Moore. The farm given him by his father, John Perkins, lies on John's river, near the mouth of Wilson's creek, just north of the "Old Oaks"-"Valley Farm" plantations of John Perkins, Jr. It is and was a very rich and valuable farm and, with the exception of a small share, now belongs intact to a grandson, who recently optioned the place to the Southern Power Company for $80,000. Mr. Perkins, like his father, took much interest in fine horses and stock in general and raised race-horses, which he ran on his own race-track, a practice very common with wealthy farmers of his day. His manner of life was very much such as is commonly understood to have been that of the typical old "country gentleman" of England in the 18th century—fox-hunting, horse-racing, good living generally, etc. His plantation was never formally named, but for many years has been popularly known as the "Aleck Perkins old place." A characteristic story is told of him: He was convoying on horseback a big four-horse wagon load of some farm product which his servants were driving down to the old Fairfield store, near where Lenoir now stands. When they arrived at the ford of a creek near Mary's Grove, the home of his brother-in-law, Parson Miller, the team was stalled and there was trouble in making it pull out of th eford. In the effort to extricate the wagon Mr. Perkins is reported to have sworn roundly at the horses, when Parson Miller, who had arrived on the scene, remonstrated. "Tut, tut, Alexander; I am surprised that a man of your age and profession should be betrayed into profanity." "Well, pray 'em out, please!" was the quick retort. He left the following children:

Clarissa, married twice, first to Thomas D. Horton, and, second, to J. J. Presnell, who died childless.

Theodore resigned immediately after graduating from West Point and married, but died early. He left one daughter, Clara, a beautiful girl, who soon after graduating from St. Mary's Raleigh, and did not long survive.

Theddeus, to whose heirs the whole of the estate fell, died before his father, and his son, Thaddeus, having bought the share of his brother Thomas and part of his brother Allison's share, owns the bulk of the "Aleck Perkins old place." He is rich, is one of Caldwell county's leading citizens and has the following family: Robert Perkins, wh ois prospering in Beunos Aires, Argentina; ——— Perkins, living in Colorado; Samuel ("Si") Perkins, an A. and E. graduate, a scientific expert in the Bureau of Soils, Agricultural Department, Washington; Ernest Perkins, at one time farm demonstrator for Burke; George Perkins, member of the Caldwell Board of Education, and living at home and assisting his father in conducting the farm; Clara, unmarried, at the head of the house; Susan, married to Dr. Thomas of Thomasville.

(8) Sarah Perkins.
Sarah Perkins married Thomas Snoddy of Surry. No information as to them is at hand; it is believed that they moved to Virginia.

(9) Eli Perkins.
Born Dec. 27, 1777, Eli Perkins died unmarried, but the date of his demise is not known. All that is known is that he resided at his father's home at Island Ford, and by tradition he is credited with having been very amiable in disposition but debited with a tendency toward convivial habits. In those days, and, indeed, in other days, conviviality was not always discouraged as much as it should have been, and in the case of Eli Perkins, tradition says, this habit received encouragement from a very dangerous source. He had a negro servant to wait upon him, whose only service appears to have been to act as body servant to his master, and this negro dearly loved his dram. Not content to leave his master to his own devices in the matter of drinking, this negro's own thirst caused him frequently to remind his master of a thirst he might have forgotten but for his insinuatingly asking: "Marse Eli, isn't you gittin' sorter dry?" We know how inaccurate tradition often is and how it has passed opened up the wrong trail in more than one instance in the history of John Perkins; so I do not give much credence to this story, but believe it is simply a survival of a broad species of "joshing" the boys perpetrated upon Eli to give him the "grins" and perhaps to cause him to think twice before imbibing once. At any rate, he was a very popular member of his father's family and his visits from Island Ford to his four brothers on John's river always ranked with the coming of Christmas among the juvenile members of those four families, who placed "Uncle Eli" on a pedestal equal in altitude to that of Santa Claus. In each of the three succeeding generations Eli Perkins had namesakes and his brother-in-law, Parson Miller, named one of his sons for him. One seldom names a son for a person for whom one has no esteem. A peculiar fact in this connection is that not one of these namesakes lived to be married. (1) Parson Miller's son, Eli Washington, born Nov. 26, 1802, died unmarried in 1820. (2) Major Elisha Perkins Miller's son, Eli Perkins Miller, born in 1823, died unmarried in 1853. However, the date had been fixed for his marriage to a charming lady who remained unmarried until her death within the last ten years. (3) Major Miller's grandson, Robert Eli Scott, son of Dr. and Mrs. W. W. Scott, born in 1857, died before he was a year old.

PART III.
MARY'S GROVE AND VALLE CRUCIS

The object of this paper is two-fold:

(1) Covering a period of 75 years, beginning 130 years ago, viz., from

1787 to 1861, to depict the average style and manner of life of a family residing in the upper Piedmont section, close to the mountains, in western North Carolina, and belonging to what may be called, for lack of a better word, the "upper class." During this period there were two heads of the family, the father, who established Mary's Grove, and his son, who succeeded him. The former, who was master of Mary's Grove for 47 years, from 1787 to 1834, was a clergyman and a missionary as well as a pioneer, and the standard of living established by him was not so typical of the standard prevailing in the more settled sections of the State as was that followed by his son from 1834 to 1861. To be sure, there was hospitality unbounded and the courtesies and amenities to be looked for from an old-fashioned gentleman, but his character as a clergyman, the scarcity of neighbors and the "backwoods" state of the country naturally produced more simplicity in the conduct of his domestic affairs than was the fashion "down the country." When the son succeeded the father times had changed, the country had been settled up and brought into communication with the rest of the State and the style of living at Mary's Grove under him may be regarded as typical of the life of a country gentleman in Piedmont North Carolina in easy circumstances but without wealth, as wealth is considered in these days. But aside from the modification of the manner of life, which was a natural development due to the progress of civilization, it may be assumed that the simplicity and lack of ostentation which distinguished the establishment under the father prevailed also under the son, although the hospitality of the latter was necessarily more extensive because has was a layfan, a man of affairs, a politician and owned a racing stable.

(2) To trace an intimate relation existing between the family at Mary's Grove and the "religious house" at Valle Crucis, the establishment of which by Bishop Ives is a very romantic, interesting and tragical episode in the history of western North Carolina.

Mary's Grove Daybook

There has been preserved an old Mary's Grove record book, stained and yellowed by time, in which have been set down items indicating activities in farming, stock-raising, blacksmithing, wagon-making, gold-mining and raising thoroughbred horses. The record is confined principally to transactions of the years 1833 and 1834 and is made in the name of Mary's Grove, which is used as a clearing house, accounts being kept with Elisha P. Miller, the proprietor, and other individuals, with the blacksmith shop, with the wagon shop, with the farm, with the gold mine, with the stables. On the last page of the book is a sort of appendix in the nature of a studbook or schedule of the horses in the racing stables for the year 1837, together with accounts of the achievements of individual horses for that and previous years.

Nathaniel (Natty) Coffey was the farm overseer, in direct control of the negroes; Isaac Mathis was head blacksmith, with Allen Kilgrove and ――― Wilson assistants and "strikers;" John Stokes was woodworker and wagon-maker and, being, a family man, furnished board and lodging to the smiths, which was not exorbitant, as there is a credit given to Stokes for five months' board of Mathis, $18.75. The record incidentally furnishes Kilgrove with the character of a credible witness, for on April 5, 1833, there is a charge of $1 made against William Collins for "cash lent at muster (in presence of Allen Kilgrove.)" The blacksmith shop is charged with bar-iron in 1833 for quantities from 200 to 800 pounds at 5 cents per pound, and in 1834 for a ton at 4 cents per pound; cast steel, 30 cents; borax, 50 cents; deerskin for Kilgrove's apron, 88 cents; two days' hauling coal-wood, negro and oxen, $1.50; 20 cords coal-wood bought at 37½ cents per cord.

Stokes, the wagon-maker and lodging-house keeper, is charged with beef at 2½ cents per pound, except for "stall-fed" beef, which is 3 cents; pork at 4½ cents; brandy at 62½ cents per gallon (12½ cents below the market price of 75 cents); cotton at 16 2-3 cents per pound, if it was ginned, but much higher if it was in the seed; half a mutton, $1; flour at 3½ cents per pound; to cash at show, 25 cents; to cash at muster to pay tax, $1; and credit by woodwork on wagons at $20 each. (These are simply specimens of charges and credits, showing prices prevailing in 1833-4.) Kilgrove is charged with cash at show, 50 cents; at shooting match, 50 cents; at election, 68¾ cents.

The individuals with whom accounts were kept lived, within a radius of ten miles, in an area of approximately 225 square miles, and their indebtedness was, for the most part, due to the blacksmith and wagon-maker. The handiwork of such artisans was, in those days, most hand-made and there was little or no importation. The items abound with charges that sound strange and even barbarous at the present day, such as "jumping" axes, "upsetting" hoes, "laying bull-tongue" plows, shoeing John Waugh's horse all round and finding iron, $1, or shoeing Mr. Laxton's horse all round, iron found, 50 cents; "steeling" an axe, putting "frizzen" on singletrees, mending bells, making bridle bits, making bell clappers. But among the debits and credits were other items besides making and mending wagons, plows and other implements and shoeing horses: To one customer was charged "cash advanced for Bishop at church, $1," to another $8 for clearing a swamp, and to still another $2.62½ for three days' "cradling" wheat—87½ cents per day! And to John Boone, nephew of Daniel Boone, was charged $50 for "one gray horse, 8 years old," which was paid for by Mr. Boone's administrator a year after his death, along with other debits. Among the items is "board of Mr. Boone's daughter while at school to 'Mr. Gates.'" The sale of the horse to Mr. Boone is the only item of transactions in horses contained in the day book, which also fails to record sales of cattle on the hoof raised on the mountain pastures. Hogs and sheep are frequently charged to individuals, the prices ranging from $1 to $3 each, "corn-cracking" pigs, six weeks old, being rated at $1 apiece. There is a record of one "Barkshire" hog being sold for $10, evidently for breeding purposes. Of the cattle, in considerable number, killed for consumption at Mary's Grove and for sale to employes and other purchasers, the hides, both "green" and "dry," were sold to Harper & Waugh, conducting extensive stores and tanneries at Fairfield, a mile away and half way between Mary's Grove and the site of what afterwards became the town of Lenoir.

John William Frederick Gates

One interesting item is the following charge against Maj. Miller's sister-in-law, who lived about 12 miles west of Mary's Grove in the western part of Burke county, near Morganton:

March, 1840. To former board of her son, 13 weeks at .75___$ 9.75
             To her part of Mr. Gates' board_____   .75
Mar. 27, 1840. To 11 weeks' board of her son at .75_____ 8.25
             To her part of Mr. Gates' board_____   .75

                                                              $19.50

Mr. Gates was a Prussian by birth who had Anglicized or Americanized the spelling of his name. It has been handed down of him that he was "highly educated," which may be true. There is evidence that he was a man of broad intelligence, of considerable force of character and well qualified as a thorough school teacher. Maj. Miller located him at Mary's Grove, built for him an "office" in the grove, consisting of a commodious school room, with quarters attached for his study and a sleeping room. Other similar one-story buildings were erected, from time to time as occasion required, for the accommodation of a limited number of girls and boys who came from a distance to attend Mr. Gates' school. These children were mostly nephews and nieces of Maj. Miller living in the upper part of Burke, near Morganton, and the sons and daughters of a few other friends like Mr. Boone. The above bill, rendered to Mrs. Mary Caldwell Perkins, of Pleasant Valley, John's river, furnishes a key to Mr. Gates' contract of employment, by which he was to receive a net sum per annum, "board and lodging found." At the beginning of a term each scholar was assessed a pro rata share of the expense of Mr. Gates' board at 75 cents per week and of his net salary. There were eight Mary's Grove children and it is easy to compute that, after boarding and lodging Mr. Gates and from half a dozen to a dozen children at 75 cents per week, the coffers of the "clearing house" would swell with the profits of each term. Of course there was a number of "day scholars."

Mr. Gates taught at Mary's Grove for several years, and what they learned from him was all "the schooling" many of his pupils ever received. He taught "the classics," Latin and Greek, some French, emphasized "the Globes" and natural history, and was especially attentive to spelling, handwriting and mathematics. He wrote a beautiful hand, as specimens still extant prove, and many is the bad quarter of an hour most of his pupils approximate the symmetrical curves of the "copy" he had given them to have spent, with heads on one side and chewing their tongues, striving to imitate. He was patient, in a degree, and conscientious effort joined to moderate improvement was apt to satisfy him, but in the long run his pupils HAD to progress. This looks like a pretty fair kind of "education." To be sure "natural science" was a sealed book and that certainly was unfortunate, but the great colleges and universities knew as little about that as he did, and the men and women he turned out could certainly spell and write, accomplishments not universal in these days of advanced systems of education. He was a severe disciplinarian and did not spare the rod.

No traditions of his pupils "locking out the Sinjin" or playing other pranks with him have come down, and his old pupils have always spoken of him with the greatest respect as "Mr. Gates;" he has never been referred to as "old man Gates."

Mr. Gates was not a jovial man, but was reserved and dignified in his manner. Whether he came to America in his early youth is not known, but his command of the English tongue was so complete that there was scarcely perceptible a foreign accent in his use of it. With all these admirable qualities he was slave to a great weakness. A reserved bachelor, he had no intimates and either affected, or allowed to grow up around him, a certain air of mystery. The same is true of a more celebrated, but not more gifted, contemporary, Peter Stewart Ney, who lived further down the country, in Rowan and Surry counties, and whose dark sayings when in his cups led those who heard him to believe he was Marshal Ney and that some one else had been shot in his place in Paris and that he had escaped to America. So much other evidence bolstered up this theory that, some twenty-odd years ago, Rev. James A. Weston, then rector of Christ church, Raleigh, N. C., wrote and published a most interesting and plausible book sustaining the thesis. Mr. Gates never touched spirits during school terms, but during vacation would frequently indulge in prolonged sprees. It was then that he, too, would whisper around dark and mysterious hints, and, whether the Peter Ney stories caused the Burke county people to build up on Mr. Gates' vaporing or whether he may have made definite claims, it began to be believed that he had been some great body in Prussia and that he was in America on account of high political reasons. What his subsequent career was is not known.

Mountain Pasture Lands

North of Mary's Grove, about 20 miles away, rises the crest of the Blue Ridge, where grass grows in the woods if only the underbrush is cut away and the sun allowed to slant in between the limbs of the trees. As far back as 1833 a great deal of these mountain lands could be "entered" and granted by the State for a small sum per acre or could be purchased from grantees for as little as a dollar an acre, so that the possession of large areas of land was not an indication of wealth unless the owner was energetic enough to improve it. The virgin growth of valuable timber was considered of no value and was regarded as a disadvantage, the cost of clearing the land and fitting it for pasturage and meadow being many times greater than that of purchase. Maj. Miller acquired about two sections of this land, on both sides of the Blue Ridge, at what is now the popular summer resort of Blowing Rock. It was then in Ashe county, now in Watauga. Ample pastures and meadows were prepared, and here during the grazing season large herds of Durham cattle and a good many of his fine horses were pastured. As the grazing season neared its close the cattle ready for market were in prime condition and were sold to the southern drovers and butchers. The dry cows at Mary's Grove were driven up and their places taken by others that had become milkers during the summer. These dry cows and what remained of the mountain herd went into winter quarters and were fed upon the best of timothy hay and the grain that had been raised on the mountain land for them. This was principally rye, although a limited quantity of a small and hardy kind of corn was raised. Ordinary large-grained, large-eared corn could not be grown in the mountains in those early years, although it flourishes there now. The hardiest brood mares, colts and yearlings were also stabled for the winter on the mountain farm, while the finest and most promising of the horses and those that needed pampering were taken to the stables at Mary's Grove.

The Mary's Grove Durhams were splendid cattle and one of the members of the original herd, "Violet" by name, lived to a great age, the writer of this having seen her when he was a boy, sporting copper rings in her horns as accompaniments to a blue ribbon awarded her by a New York State fair association. She was a gift to Maj. Miller from Bishop Ives. The strain of the breed still exists in Caldwell county. The line of descent of a certain family was carefully preserved up to fifteen years ago, when the individuals were as perfect Jerseys in appearance as if they had been full bloods. Except from a sentimental point of view, the Durham blood had "run out."

Apropos of the cheapness of land in the old days is this story of an East Tennessean who owned a mountain farm and a valley plantation and wanted to sell out and go to Texas. He found a purchaser for the valley plantation and, after "passing the deed" and receiving his money, went home and said that he owned no land in Tennessee at last and could move to Texas in peace. But, he was reminded, he had only sold the valley plantation. "'Sh! Not a word till I get out of the State; I slipped the mountain farm into the deed and he don't know it!"

The Miller Gold Mine

Some years prior to 1833 Judge Anderson Mitchell, Col. Richard Venable Michaux, Alexander Perkins, Esq., and Maj. Elisha P. Miller became joint owners of a gold mining "prospect" located on a branch in the small mountains about ten miles west of Mary's Grove. Finally Maj. Miller became sole owner. When developed it was a placer mine in which the gold was "washed" out or "panned" out from the sand or soil according to the primitive methods of placer mining. It was never a brilliant financial success, although there was always enough tantalizing promise in it for it to have remained a Mary's Grove property for over thirty years, and as it was popularly spoken of as a "paying" mine it is probable that it netted an annual income of between four and five hundred dollars. One trouble about such mines was that they were generally rented out to practical miners who paid a toll of one-fifth of the gross output and the question always bobbed up— Is it one-fifth? The miners in charge were frequently changed, and it was probably a mistake that this was so. The only records in the Mary's Grove Day Book of the proceeds of the gold mine are for the period from Feb. 1 to June 30, 1833, five months, and from June 1 to Sept. 9, 1835, three and a third months, and these returns are taken as a measure of the returns for future years, the popular impression that the mine was a "paying" proposition rendering this estimate plausible:

(1) During 81 working days—for often for weeks at a time no work

was done—of these five months, 1,230 pennyweights of gold were taken out, the average per day being 15.18 pennyweights; the highest per diem was 24.16 pennyweights and the lowest 7. The gold was 80 cents the pennyweight—now it is $1.—and this output of 1,230 pennyweights for five months was worth $984; toll of one-fifth of this is $196.80, or $39.36 per month, making an annual toll, upon this basis, of $472.32.

(2) The returns made for the period from June 1 to Sept. 9, 1835, cover only toll, and eight reports aggregate 241 pennyweights of toll gold for 3 1-3 months, making 72.3 pennyweights, or $57.84 per month—$694.08 per annum.

(3) Adding the annual toll of the five months' report ($472.32) and the annual toll of the three and one-third months report (694.80) gives $1,166.40, which, divided by two, makes $583.20 as a general average annual toll. The annual toll of $583.20 is 6 per cent on $9,720, and if any such income did continue to be received it is not surprising that the property was held for over thirty years, even if it may have been suspected that it was not paying as much as it ought to have paid.

A few years after the close of the civil war, between 1867 and 1870, there was quite a gold-mining excitement in this section of North Carolina, and a corporation chartered outside of the State purchased Pax Hill gold mine, a "prospect" only that had never been developed, located on a neighboring branch to that of the Miller mine, for $50,000, paying $25,000 down. Very soon after this transaction some company, possibly the same one that had bought Pax Hill, offered the administrator of Maj. Miller's estate $20,000 for the Miller mine. Pax Hill had never been worked and the Miller mine had and was known to be a "paying" proposition and naturally the administrator desired to receive at least as much for his mine as had been paid for Pax Hill. He was sure, he almost knew, his mine was a better one than Pax Hill. He refused to take $20,000 and held out for more. Before a great while the purchasers of Pax Hill convinced themselves that their mine had a few extraordinarily rich "pockets" which they had rifled, but that they could find no more; so they defaulted on their second payment of $25,000. And the Miller mine, for which $20,000 had been offered, was later sold for $700.

Race Horses

Although more than 50 years had elapsed since the formal separation of the American colonies from the British government, the British passion for the race-course still existed in North Carolina, along with the rooted conviction that it was the duty of every country gentleman to do his part in keeping the blooded stock of horses up to the standard. There was nothing in this akin to modern Anglomania, for it was bred in the bone and the North Carolinians were not conscious of aping the English, but considered it part of their inheritance, like Magna Carta. "Other times, other customs." It is difficult, at this stage of modern utilitarian development, to fully understand how, from sixty to a hundred years ago, upwards of 25 gentlemen of moderate means, and engaged in agriculture in the counties of Burke and Wilkes, should have considered it their duty to keep from

25 to 50 thorough/brd horses and colts mewed up in stables, eating their heads off and doing nothing but running a race now and then—just to improve the stock! But so it was, and Maj. Miller was one of the enthusiastic patrons of the turf, as is evidenced by the following extract from page 143 of Mary's Grove Day Book:

Stud of E. P. Miller, Burke County, 1837-8

No. 1—Bertrand, the Younger, 7 years old, by Bertrand, Senior, dam by Virginius.

No. 2—Polly Morgan, 3 years old, sorrel filly, by Monsieur Tonson, dam by Timoleon.

No. 3—Diana, 12 years old, sorrel mare, by Perkins' Florizel, he by imported Diomed, her dam by Sir Harry, by imported Sir Harry, etc.

No. 4—Kitty Smith, bay mare, by Blackburn's Whip, dam by Medley.

No. 5—Mountain Maid, bay filly, by Andrew of Tennessee, dam Kitty Smith.

No. 6—Black Betty, pedigree not known.

No. 7—Blue Hawk, 3 years old, bay colt, by Perkins' Riott, dam Black Betty.

No. 8—Pigeon, brown mare, by Sudderth's Citizen, dam not known.

No. 9—Smiling Billy, two years old, sorrel colt by Bertrand, dam Blaze of Gallatin.

No. 10—Sally Ridge, bay filly by Bertrand, dam Pigeon.

No. 11—Maid of Norway, brown filly, out of Black Betty, by Daniel Morgan, he by Heazein, he by Sir Archy.

No. 12—Talapoosa, sorrel colt, by Daniel Morgan, dam Blaze by Gallatin.

No. 13—Paugus, bal colt, by Bertrand, dam Pigeon.

No. 14—Mary McDowell, sorrel filly, by Bertrand, dam Sleep Kate, by bay Diomed, grand dam by imported President.

No. 15—Lucy Forrester, 6 years old, bay mare, by Marshal Ney, by John Richard, by old Sir Archy; her dam by Carolinian, by imported True Blue. Lucy Forrester was raised by ex-Governor Hutchings G. Burton and sold to W. J. Alexander of Lincoln, who sold a half interest in the mare to E. P. Miller.

No. 16—Osceola, chestnut sorrel colt, by Singleton's Godolphin, dam Lucy Forrester.

No. 17—Isola, bay filly, by Bertrand, dam Lucy Forrester.

No. 18—Roxanna, bay filly, by Bertrand, dam Black Betty.

No. 19—Little Jim, sorrel colt, by Bertrand, dam Diana.

No. 20—Big Jim, sorrel colt, by Bertrand, dam Kitty Smith.

The above paraphrase of jockey jargon would be almost as unintellible, without translation, to the generality of people nowadays as baseball lingo would have been to our predecessors of 1837, but to them it was not only intelligible but intensely interesting as having relation to the history and accomplishments of an equine aristocracy in which these horses held, locally at least, distinguished station.

The record shows the following gentlemen who traded, trafficked and crossed stock with the Mary's Grove stables: Robert Simonton, who owned

Gallatin; James Erwin, who imported and owned Meteor; John Perkins, who owned Florizel; Alexander Perkins, who owned Riott; John Sudderth, who owned Citizen; Barlett Shipp, Gen. Lowdermilk, Dr. Satterwhite, Dr. Jones, Capt. McDowell, W. J. Alexander, R. M. Pearson and others. There was great rivalry and difference of opinion as to superiority of stock among the partisans of Gallatin, Florizel, Riott, Citizen and Bertrand, but the acutest divergence was between the Citizen and Bertrand adherents, the Sudderth darkeys swearing by Citi-zen while the Mary's Grove negroes bet all their money on "Bertram."

Ellen White, a fine 3-year-old filly, was sold out of the stud in 1836 to Judge Strange for $150. Blaze, "the Bowman mare," had also been sold out of the stud but left two colts in it, Smiling Billy and Talapoosa. She was sold as a filly for $85 and bought for Mary's Grove for $110. The record does not state what the Mary's Grove stables got for her. (These prices show that thoroughbred stock did not sell at exorbitant rates.) There are a number of other horses, colts and fillies that had been sold, but no other prices are given.

Only four races are recorded:

(1) May, 1837, Polly Morgan won a sweepstakes in Morganton, purse $137.50, entrance fee $25, beating Capt. McDowell's Lance filly, Alexander Perkins' Riott filly, Isaac West's Field filly and a South Carolina horse belonging to Mr. Little, Polly carrying nine pounds over weight. Polly Morgan was a red sorrel and was bought from Capt. Moody in Raleigh in 1836.

(2) October 10, 1837. At Morganton she beat Capt. McDowell's Lance filly and Alexander Perkins' Peter Pinder by Riott, she carrying 18 pounds over weight. Entrance fee $50.

(3) At same time and place she was beaten in two heats, of one mile each, by A. Sherrill's Riott filly, one heat "from the throat-latch out" and the other by half a length. "It was believed she would have distanced the filly if she had carried equal weight." (A case of too much jockey.) These were all mile heats and Polly's distance is two miles." (No quarter horse.)

(4) Ran Polly Morgan at Wilkesborough, November, 1837, two miles heats against Gen. Lowdermilk's Monsieur Tonson, 4-year-old horse, and against Bogle's colt. She distance the field with ease under a hard pull.

This is a transcript of the account of four races that has been preserved out of a record covering a racing-stable career extending over 20 years into the future from a date when the stables and Polly Morgan were of the same age—about three years old; the remaining portions of the record, if available, would show many victories (and some defeats) in notable events in which the redoubtable Polly and the other horses in the stable took part; for Polly Morgan and others of her colleagues made great reputations in racing circles. In the two heats in which Sherrill's Riott filly beat her once "from the throat-latch out" and again "by half a length," her fat jockey should have paraphrased Tennyson and encouraged her, in the second heat at least, by crying out, "Half a length, half a length, half a length onward!"

A horse having the pedigree, appearance and qualities of the three-year-year bay filly, Ellen White, sold to Judge Strange in 1836 for $150, would sell today for not less than $1,000, and probably for $1,500.

The record speaks of a fine mare, Arabia by name, the property of Judge Pearson, who rusticated, during the summer of 1837, on the mountain pasture at Blowing Rock. Fellow-guests with Arabia were a gray mare and her thoroughbred colt, Grampus, the property of Bartlett Shipp of Lincoln. Mr. Shipp, a respected friend and honored guest at Mary's Grove, was cousin and guardian of Lucy K. Abernethy, who became the wife of Robert C. Miller, Maj. Miller's eldest son, and was also a cousin of Nancy Abernethy, the wife of John Perkins, Jr., Maj. Miller's uncle. A kinsman of the Mary's Grove family used to make the whimsical complaint that they liked Mr. Shipp better than any of their kinspeople and that, when they spoke of "Mr. Shipp," they employed a tone of voice like that of the wife of a second lieutenant in the army or an ensign in the navy when she called her husband "Mr.," as if he were just a little better kind of "Mr." than the ordinary "Mr." This was an inherited friendship, for Parson Miller was very fond of Bartlett Shipp and his forbears. Still, he could not always have his way with his young friend Bartlett, for the correspondence between Bishop Ravenscroft and Parson Miller shows that these Reverend and Right Reverend gentlemen endeavored unsuccessfully to induce Bartlett Shipp and Robert Burton to become Episcopal lay-readers in Lincoln.

Commingling notices of horses and people is proper, for the horse is a noble animal and the friendship between the thoroughbred and his master is very fond and their relations close and intimate. Doubtless Gov. Burton of Halifax took pride in having raised aristocratic Lucy Forrester, and her subsequent owners, W. J. Alexander and E. P. Miller, were not less proud of the glory she and her progeny brought to their stables or of the profit they put in their pockets. Mr. Alexander was grandfather of the beautiful and talented Miss Laura Alexander, who was one of the first of the women of North Carolina to break an old tradition in entering a public profession; for soon after the civil war she went upon the stage, and her no less beautiful and charming aunt, Miss "Coosie" Wilson, beloved and admired in all that section, went with her as a companion and was her niece's chaperon during her theatrical career. Thus it appears that with the passing of the old regime the character of racing changed and the thoroughbred and their masters entered upon new careers involving much of practical utility and no less of high breeding.

Sired by the great Bertrand and with fast Polly Morgan for her dam, chestnut sorrel Scotia, foaled April 30, 1839, was a princess of the blood royal, so trim and dainty that she was never put upon the course, but was set aside as riding horse for the only young lady of the Mary's Grove family, which consisted of seven sons and the daughter. One afternoon, as Scotia and her young mistress were leaving Lenoir for their home at Mary's

Grove. two miles away, there rode in front of them an old citizen who sat his horse in that bending-forward, bundled-up and swaying attitude characteristic of a gentleman in his cups, and as they neared him he turned his face upward and backward and, in the most agreeable and sociable, if somewhat tipsy, manner, called out, "Whip up, my good gal! We're both both going the same way." The "good gal' took him at his word and a gentle touch of the crap on Scotia's flank was all the hint she needed to show her heels and burn the wind. Scotia had been unsaddled and unbridled and had wallowed, and had about finished cropping all the grass she cared for on the lawn, when she raised her head and whinnied a derisive hello at the inebriated citizen and his nag as they jogged and nodded along down the road.

Personal Recollections

A grandson who was eight years old when Maj. Miller died in 1861 has some charming childish recollections of Mary's Grove during the last years of the old regime. A recent visit to the old place afforded him food for interesting philosophical reflection. Only four things remained as they appeared to him in his childhood—the graveyard (which is his own property); the grove, still beautiful but depleted; the old well, and the door that opened into "grandmother's sitting room;" though even the grove and the graveyard are changed. The old door, with its curious little metal knob and catches and its quaint battens, was one that Parson Miller had placed in the old house when it was built in 1806, and, long before it began to open up the pleasures of childhood to the philosophizing visitor, it had swung upon its hinges for the frequent comings and goings of Bishop Ravenscroft, Bishop Ives, Bishop Atkinson, Bishop Green, John Henry Hobart, Dr. Buxton, Dr. Thurston, Dr. Gries and scores of other ecslesiastical and lay worthies. When the old house was torn down, many years ago, the then owner, perhaps for sentimental reasons, saved this door and had it set in a doorway of the new house built upon the old site. The present owner, with rare generosity, has given the door to the whilom small boy, who has replaced it with a modern shutter.

This boy's recollection is that in Bertrand's stead another Sultan reigned, a fine black-bay named Puzzle, who lived in solemn, stately seclusion in a stable built for him on the lower borders of the limbertwig orchard, where Perry, in charge of the horses, cared for him and caressed him. Old Perry, good old black Perry—it was the joy of his heart to lead Puzzle two miles to Lenoir, on court days and other public days, for the purpose of parading him before the gaze of an admiring audience, the bestowal of whose praise upon the horse was as the oil of gladness to Perry. The boy remembers distinctly seeing the horses in the stables and hearing the race-course talk of the negroes, but he does not remember ever having seen a race or knowing anything about one. It is quite evident that during the first six years of his life he was too small to be taken to the races and, whether there were any races then or not, he would have no recollections concerning them. The same is probably true of him, from the age of six to eight years, though it is very probable that in those years, owing to the distracted state of public opinion, the minds of the community were set upon things more serious than horse-racing and that there were no races.

Fox Hounds and Game Chickens

The man, to whom the boy referred to is father, never hears a "jar-fly," that big locust whose raucous, strident scream from the great oaks is accounted portentous of hot, dry weather, or tee chanting of myriads of swamp frogs, but he thinks of Mary's Grove. His way of getting to Mary's Grove was generally this: His grandfather, bestriding his horse, whose head is turned homeward from Lenoir, in the afternoon, reaches down and, grasping him by the left arm near the shoulder, lifts him up behind, on the horse, where he sticks, like a toad on a tussock, holding on grimly to his grandfather's coat-skirts. This is often not accomplished without earnest material protests which fill the urchin's heart with misgivings but do not seem to move the grandsire at all; and what can one do under such distressing circumstances? Soon, however, the spirit of depression departs and the pleasant prospects and happy greetings on the road bring back cheerfulness and the joy of life. As the way shortens, as the westering sun declines and as the dark shadows of the grewsome grove envelop them, every oak furnishes a jar-fly who joins his fellows in sawing out a savage symphony and the frogs in the meadow take up the refrain and sing a funeral dirge. It is then that the little lad first learns what vanity of vanities means and realizes the futility of all human endeavor without maternal supervision, and, shamefacedly but sincerely, he weeps against his grandfather's back. But, hark! More cheerful sounds are heard. The hounds come trooping out, barking and baying around their master in welcoming chorus; the little darkeys, scampering from the nearby quarters, run an Olympic race in noisy competition, the goal being opening the gate for "Ole Marse;" the cheerful, ruddy lights of candles and hickory log fires emanating through the doors and windows enliven the scene, and by the time the small boy falls into grandmother's arms and is hugged and kissed and patted upon the cheek and called "little tackey" by her, his tears are dry and the world has become new and fresh and beautiful again. Where to go and what to do next is the problem. And he fears the edict that it is too late to go anywhere out of doors, for he had been counting on a round of the quarters with his favorites among the young darkeys and a visit to Uncle Jim to see the 'possum he has fattening and to learn what progress Joe is making at putting a new handle in the small boy's miniature axe. There were other things it would be very agreeable to do also, as visiting the stables, examining the chicken runs, etc., but they would "keep" till morning, especially as he was sure that out of seven uncles there would be enough at home to furnish him with choice diversion between supper and bedtime. Much as he loved and admired his grandfather, who was something of a valetudinarian at this time, he had no patience with his imples diet of mush and milk, followed by hot corn pone and butter and a glass of milk; so he contrived to be seated at the supper table near his grandmother and regaled himself on the more toothsome dainties with which she provided him. After supper everybody repaired to "the hall," in the wide fireplace of which a big log fire was blazing, the grandmother, who always wore a "cap," sitting in one corner knitting (the most suitable diversion for a lady at night when the brightest light was that afforded by tallow candles and pine-knots), while the grandfather sat in the other corner reading the National Intelligencer, which was not the easiest thing in the world for an old gentleman, as was indicated by his frequent "snuffing" of the candles. (People in those days seem to have eaten a great deal more beef than they do nowadays, and the question is raisd whether they did not butcher the beeves, as much as for any other reason, to obtain tallow for candles! The small boy seems to remember seeing candle "moulds" always in process of being strung with wicks, of having the melted tallow poured in the dozen cylinders of each mould and of being hung out in cool places to harden. The long winter nights were the cause of the burning up and melting of millions of candles.) Be that as it may, the boy was soon deeply interested in more or less veracious stories of hunting, fishing and riding, and of the prodigies performed by the various animals engaged in the chase and race, which his uncles laid themselves out to relate for his entertainment. One of these uncles, who allowed himself to be monopolized and tyrannized over by him, was full of folk-lore and woods-lore, was weather-wise and knew all about animals, birds and fishes. He was a modern Will Honeycombe, without his vagrant habits. It is true that he divided his time largely between Mary's Grove, the gold mine and the mountain farm. The gold mine and the mountain farm were both located, by the small boy's imagination, in the realm of romance and mystery. The gold mine, he was sure, was the residence of Aladdin and his wonderful lamp, and he had a great longing to visit the mountain farm, for "Sairy in the Mountains," a negro woman who cooked at the mountain farm, and who from time to time came to Mary's Grove for a change, had given him accounts, exaggerated no doubt, of the broad acres in meadow and pasture, of the vast droves of horses and herds of cattle on the pastures and of the grand scenery. Later his strong desire to go to "the mountains" was gratified and he visited the mountain farm and Valle Crucis. He has vague memories of horses, cattle, mountains massed upon mountains and distant views, but the only really distinct recollection he has is that of seeing a huge rattlesnake which his uncle, who owned Valle Crucis, kept in a box with a glass window, together with deer horns stuck around the walls and bear skins spread on the floors. Dried venison hams and "mountain sugar" made from maple syrup also rise up out of the indistinctness and claim a place in memory. The boy was allowed to "sit up" till all the family went to bed and the excitements of the afternoon and evening had only the effect of closing his little eyes in draemless slumber as soon as he was well tucked in. In the middle of the night he was waked by strains of music he recognized as the winding of the hunters' horn rounding up the hounds for a fox-chase, and Loud, Lumber, Music and all the pack responded in joyful chorus of baying up and down the gamut, from the treble of Music to the deep bass of old Lumber. A few sharp halloos from "the boys" got the hounds well in hand and presently they speeded, yelping, barking, baying, off and away toward the forest. The stories the little boy had heard made him familiar with every move to be made—circling and hunting, with a yelp of encouragement now and then from the leaders, egged on by sharp halloos from the hunters; striking the scent and following the trail, announced by the "opening" of the leader, when the whole pack joined in a grand volume of exciting music which kept up as long as the trail was "hot" but diminished and faded away if it grew "cold," which happened if the wily fox back-tracked, doubled or took to water; then followed more hunting and long-range circling till the hot trail was picked up again; on a hot trail the concerted baying of the hounds was resumed and became one harmonious volume of concerted music as it grew hotter; no tongue or pen can describe the climax of this swelling, sonorous, bounding billow of baying, sweeping in waves through the forest, as the foremost hounds, in the ecstasy of the chase, caught the first distant, fleeting glimpse of Reynard's gray brush; soon run down and exhausted, the fox was an easy prey, for in face of a pack of hounds he could not be said to be "at bay;" the hunters tried always be keep up with the hounds by cutting across and doubling like a fox, in order to enjoy the music and excitement and to be in at the death to prevent the hounds from tearing the fox to pieces. Lying tucked away in his warm nest in bed, the little boy's imagination drew for him these exciting pictures while he listened to the music of the horns and hounds scamperng away to the forest, and, as the last faint notes of the sweet music died away, he dropped off to sleep again. As a boy and man this was as near as he ever came to being on a fox-hunt and he is well satisfied, for it took a tough, hardy youngster to keep up with the hounds in the rough woods, where "riding to the hounds" would have been out of the question. The start was at an hour anywhere from 2 a.m. until daybreak, in order to encounter the fox fresh upon his travels and to trail him when the dew was on the ground and the scent was fresh and hot.

Next morning he was up bright and early, had been all around the quarters and seen his little black friends and had examined Uncle Jim's 'possum, which was getting very fat and appeared to be quite as "sullen" as was becoming in a 'possum growing in girth and devoted to a sacrifice that was only delayed awaiting the preparedness of the accompanying sweet potatoes. Joe had given him his toy axe, newly helved, which he kept with him as closly as a little girl keeps her baby-doll, and as there was still plenty of time on his hands before the breakfast bell would ring, he was engaged in watching a function that interested him intensely. The game had been abroad in the forest in numbers that night, and the wind had been fair—that is to say it had been gentle and had not dried up the drew—and the uncles had caught two foxes between 2 o'clock and sunup, and as the last one was caught near home they, "came in." The pelts and brushes had been nailed up against he granary wall to dry and the carcases of the foxes, after having been boiled in a pot prepared for the purpose, were being cut up in proper proportions and thrown to the dogs, which caught them, as trained seals on the vaudeville stage catch pieces of fat bacon thrown to them, and devourd them greedily. A well-kept hound does not care for the raw flesh of a fox but only "picks over it." By feeding them on the well-seasoned cooked flesh they were educated to like it and their appetites joined with their natural instincts to make them eager for success in the chase. This pack, as their predecessors had been, were deer-hounds as well as fox-hounds, but as deer was less plentiful than formerly the fox was a more frequent quarry than deer. A pack of beagles was once introduced but it was soon discovered that these short-legged little hounds were fit only for rabbits, and as the rabbit, like the 'possum, was "nigger game," they were not kept busy. The little boy's uncle Will Honeycombe was something of a heretic in this particular, for he caught rabbits, generally by trapping them, for their "hams," which he dried just as venison hams are dried. Dried venison is delicious, but, by comparison, dried rabbit ham is as frog legs to mutton chops, and the small boy was never happier than when he came into possession of a "ham."

After breakfast there was much to do—visiting the stables, riding a gentle horse and so forth. But a surce of never-ending interest and entertainment was the chicken run, in which only game chickens were raised, and only one breed of them, the Arrington Games or Raleigh Reds. They were called Arrington Games because Maj. Miller got the stock from Senator Arrington of Nash, a colleague in the General Assembly and the popular and alliterative name of Raleigh Reds was given to them because the cocks were always of some shade of red in color and because Maj. Miller was supposed to have brought them with him in his hands, their legs tied together, when he returned from the Legislature at Raleigh. They were notable fighters and the stock still ranks high among the dominant breeds in this section. Besides the Mary's Grove run there were runs at the gold mine and at the mountain farm. The chickens were smaller and lighter in weight than chickens not pugilistically inclined, but those familiar with them have always maintained that no broiler was ever quite so tender and toothsome as a game spring chicken. The little boy has never to this day seen a chicken fight except as between roosters who of their own will and accord have entered upon hostilities, but in those days there is no denying that there were cocking mains held. "Other times, other customs" again comes to the rescue. It had been a strenuous day and by the time the boy had finished supper he could scarcely keep his eyelids apart, so he was put to bed and fell asleep as soon as he "touched the feathers."

After a full night's rest he rose with the sun, and it seemed to him that Mammy Sophy was just trying herself to delay having breakfast till dinner time, and after she had served it away up in the day (according to his computation), that his grandfather, who had promised to take him home after breakfast, was inventing excuse upon excuse to attend to first one trivial piece of business after another before starting. There had never been a mule or a pair of shafts at Mary's Grove and, unless you walked, the only way to get away from there was to drive a pair of horses to a buggy or carriage or to ride one. The very convenience of it made horse-back riding a common mode of transportation. At last the little boy was perched up behind his grandfather on his way to town and to his mother.

The love of the little boy for his sweet young mother and her love for him—what can measure it? At the first sight of her dear face such a great joy entered into his heart that it could not hold it and he fell into her arms and sobbed upon her breast, and she fondled and caressed him and mingled her tears wtih his. Then they loved each other back to joy and gladness and lightness of heart and the world was bright and happy again for both.

Negroes at Mary's Grove

There were never very many negroes at Mary's Grove. The first census—that of 1780—credits Parson Miller with two; his father-in-law, John Perkins, a wealthy planter of Lincoln county, with thirteen, and Gen. William Lenoir, a rich Wilkes county planter on the Yadkin, with twelve. Not at this early date or at any future period was there the necessity, on the western farms, for the large number of negroes that were required on the large tobacco and cotton plantations in the central and eastern parts of the State.

At Mary's Grove a ten-acre swamp in the "bottom land" on Lower creek was given to the negroes, upon condition that they cleared it and ditched it and brought it into cultivation, for their own, and this lot of land, the richest part of the Mary's Grove bottoms, was called "Nigger Bottom" and remained theirs as long as the negroes remained at Mary's Grove. Every Saturday afternoon was a negro holiday, which they devoted, as occasion demanded, to the cultivation of their plot of ground. From the personal recollection of a very small boy the names of twenty of the Mary's Grove negroes are recalled at the time of "the surrender," not including a number of youngsters then on the place and several who had been sold by the executors of the estate at the beginning of the civil war. These facts would indicate that, in its most flourishing state, Mary's Grove was the home of about forty negroes, as the "Nigger Bottom" would have furnished a quarter of an acre apiece to forty men, women and children.

The transactions by the executors were made to accomplish two results—to meet the exigencies of debt and the bring families together. For instance, Mammy Sophy's husband did not belong to Mary Grove, but to another family, and upon occasion he was furnished with a "pass" which authorized him to go and pass the week-end, from Saturday at noon until Monday morning, at "wife's house." The pass was recognized as placing the bearer outside the category of contraband wanderers by the patrol (pattyroller). Mammy Sophy and others in like condition were transferred to the families of their husbands.

The week-ends were always happy times, extending from Saturday at noon to bedtime Sunday night, except when the cultivation of "Nigger Bottom" required the services of the working force on Saturday afternoon, and the presence of visitors added to the pleasure. Through his mind's eye the white boy looks back and reviews the childish sports of himself and his black playmates, hunting, fishing and "playing" on many a Saturday half-holiday, and he sees at night an outdoor congregation in the quarters gathered to witness, sometimes by the light of pine-knot bonfires, the graceful dancing of the larger boys and younger men to the music of a banjo or an old fiddle, accompanied by the patting of Juba by the spectators—"Juba dis and Juba dat, Juba kill de ole black cat." Each of half a dozen dusky youngsters was showing his skill at buck-dancing, double-shuffling, pigeon-winging, and their swaying bodies and rapid movements presented a picture of natural grace, when, at the magic cry of "Whing!" from the leader, they all fell into a frantic break-down, the music of their feet keeping time with that of the banjo and the patting of Juba, which was redoubled by the audience and accompanied by spirited singing:

> 'S I's gwine down t'e harves' fiel'
> Black-snake nip be on 'e heel—
> JUMP! Jim Crow.
>
> Run, niger, run—
> Pattyroller ketch you—
> Run, niger, RUN!

All this was senseless, of course, but it contributed to the gayety of the occasion; and the small boy, who has since seen George Primrose and Billy West at their best, looks back upon these darkey buck-dances and their accompaniments as equal to anything Terpsichore ever achieved.

Generally, on Sunday morning,s they were gathered in "the hall," where "Ole Miss" read from the Bible and the Prayer Book to them and the children were taught the catechism, after which they were free to do as they pleased within certain limits; the horses and cattle were to be attended to and firewood provided. It was harder on the cooks than on anybody else, but it was managed by relaying to give even the cooks a couple of Sundays a month off. All baptisms and most marriages were performed by Episcopal ministers and a few of the negroes had been confirmed and were communicants of the Episcopal Church, but the majority of them were inclined to the Methodist Church.

The obsolete law or regulation forbidding the teaching of reading and writing to negroes was a dead-letter so far as the house-servants were concerned, and the lad of reminiscences recalls two negro girls (chambermaid and nurse), a good deal older than himself, who were learning to spell and read while he was being taught his "A B C's',, and he has a clear recollection of the deep interest shown on their faces as they heard read aloud the remarkable adventures of Capitola, Old Hurricane and the bad desperadoes in Mrs. Southworth's "Hidden Hand," set forth in the "palpitating pages" of the New York Ledger. They also manifested an interest, but not so absorbing, in Porte Crayon's description of Southern travel in Harper's Magazine.

Uncle Jim and Aunt Airy claimed to be over a hundred years old, and they looked it. The boy was deeply impressed by Uncle Jim's legs, his lower extremities, which were swollen—not from dropsy—and which he always kept swathed and bandaged and pervaded by a pleasant arodatic odor of liniment, a whiff of which even to this day always brings up memories of Uncle Jim and his big bundles of legs. There was a strong bond of attachment between the boy and these old negroes, who loved to talk to him, and he delighted to listen to them. He remembers no set stories about animals, such as Uncle Remus told Miss Sally's little boy, but the line of personification of animals and of giving them the power of speech that ran through those stories was a thread ravelled out of the weave of negro fancy, and the stories sound perfectly natural to the old-time negroes and white folks of the South. The boy would sit and listen to Uncle Jim by the hour—and so did Aunt Airy, whose talk was generally inconsequential to the little boy's ears—but he remembers now actually only one thing the old man said, although he remembers that with distinctness. Uncle Jim had belonged in his youth to a man who lived to a great age, for whom he had great respect and stories about whom he never tired of telling. Of one of these stories about his old "Marster"—for Jim, as did all the negroes, used the broad "a" in pronouncing Master—only an insignificant portion is remembered in detail. He told of his master becoming exasperated over some state of affairs (which Uncle Jim recounted circumstantially), and with great vehemence exclaiming "Splud!" The youthful listener's curiosity to know what this mysterious expletive meant was gratified only to the extent of Uncle Jim's declaring that he did not know the meaning of it and that it was only a "byword" anyhow. Years after, during the reading of Shakespeare of some other book, dealing with life in England two hundred years or more ago, the appearance on a page of " 'S blood" brought up beside it, in memory, "Splud" and Uncle Jim! Uncle Jim'se old master used the old, obsolete and archaic English expletive, " 'S blood!" in Jim's presence, who repeated it phonetically and to the mystification of his youthful listener. This opened up another fanciful bit of philosophizing. If Jim was a hundred years old and if his old master had also lived to be a hundred years old and if Jim had been fifteen years old when his old master died, the latter would have been ten years old when King Charles the Second died. And that was the age when the expletive " 'S blood!" was in most common use, for upon the accession of William and Mary it soon became archaic and fell into disuse. So, upon the above assumptions, the whilom youth worked it out that he had spoken with a man who had spoken with another man who might have spoken with King Charles the Second!

Old as she was, Aunt Airy was not responsible for the remark made by a centenarian in another family, who certainly looked what she claimed to be—much more than a hundred years old. One of her "white folks," in conversation with her, adverted to the fact of her having reached a ripe old age. "Yes'm, Miss Mary, I sho' is been here a long spell; but, Miss Mary," and spoke in an awed tone in which there was real pathos and none of the characteristic negro whimsicalities, "I sometimes thinks maybe the Lord's forgot me!"

Old Lawson Michaux, while not a Mary's Grove negro, belonged to another branch of the Perkins family residing on John's river in Burke county, and his son, "young" Lawson, walked in the tracks of his respected parent and gave his sons and daughters the names of good people. He had nine sons and two daughters and, after naming one of the sons Lawson, for his father (and himself), he called the eight others George Folk, Clinton Cilley,

Gray Bynum, Burgess Gaither, Alphonso Avery, Nicholas Woodfin, Wade Hampton and Grover Cleveland, the names of eight men much respected in North Carolina. Th eolder daughter was named for his sister, Minnie Lou, and when the youngest child, a daughter, was born, Lawson came down the river to tell his "young Miss," a granddaughter of Mr. Richard V. Michaux and of Maj. Miller, about her advent. "Now, Lawson," said this young lady, "you have one son named for your father, a good man, and eight other sons named for eight very eminent gentlemen; Minnie Lou is named for a good woman, and you should name this little baby for the finest and best woman in the world"——

"Yes'm, I done done so."

"——for the great and good Queen, Victoria."

"Yes'm, I knows she's a fine 'oman, but ef I names this young 'un Victo-ry she'll allus be called Vic for short; so we just named her for you, ma'am!" And so Queen Victoria was turned down and the young child was named and in the course of years was married to a young negro who bore the same name—given and sirname—that the husband of Lawson's "young Miss" bears, and the reason that the mails in that community are not badly scrambled is attributed to the fact that there is always a discreet administration of the postoffice at Adako. In justice to the black girl it must be said that she took the initiative in the matter of marriage and that she had "done got her man and gone on" before a white man of the same name as her husband "tuck and" married "young Miss."

There were always holidays given when the circus came, on election day and for one day during court week, and the negroes always attended these functions. If they did not have money of their own—and they generally had, either from the proceeds from the "Nigger Bottom" land or from the tips that they were expert in accumulating—they were given tickets to the circus, and the happiest times at the circus the small boy could have enjoyed would have been to be allowed to go with them—which he was not allowed to do! They were regular attendants at elections and on "Tuesday of court week," when Perry took Puzzle or some other high-bred stallion to parade the streets of Lenoir and to exhibit his fine qualities, he was always followed by an admiring throng of his Mary's Grove adherents ready to stake the "Bertram" stock against the "Citi-zen" or any other fine breed of horses in the State.

In the days before there were any railroads and before railroads were very common the only way of getting to market was by wagons over bad roads to Cross Keys (Fayetteville) and Charleston, and, after a railroad was built to that town, to Columbia, and of course the negroes, some of them, made these trips. And many were the wonderful stories they brought back touching their adventures on their travels. For years and years afterwards the story of the "falling stars," as related by the party out on the road in the fall of 1833, was repeated in the quarters by those who saw the phenomenon and they never quite got over the shock that came to them when they thought the end of the world was at hand. Mr. N. A. Powell, who was then a lad, was out on a trip on that occasion and he used to say it was no laughing matter to go through such an experience. The negroes had a wonderful story to tell of what they saw and heard as they traveled through the domains of the elder Wade Hampton. They said he had tried and tried to bring the number of his servants up to an even thousand, but that every time he reached that notch one would die or take to the swamps and he never could say that his people numbered a thousand. As he would be riding along the roads and would meet a negro he would say, "Whose darkey are you?" "I belongs to Marse Wade Hampton, sir." Every time that answer was made he would throw a silver dollar to the negro—a very generous if not a frugal practice.

There were loom-houses where the cloth was woven for clothing the negroes and the women, either in their cabins or this house, would card the cotton and wool and spin the rolls into thread for the use of the looms. Of course there was necessity for dyeing apparatus. As the number of servants at Mary's Grove was comparatively small, there were no skilled mechanics among them and shoemakers were hired each fall to come and take measures, "cut out" and make the season's shoes. There were enough cobblers of little skill to half-sole and mend during the winter.

There is now living on a farm that was part of the old Mary's Grove homeplace a lady who was born on the place in 1835 and since that year she has virtually lived on that farm. She was the daughter of Nathan Clark, the hatter, who cultivated some land on the Mary's Grove plantation and made wool hats. He made all the wool hats needed at Mary's Grove, and of course for all the countryside. The writer, then a boy, wore old man Nath Clark's wool hats all during the civil war. They may not have been as light or as stylish as hats he has since worn, but they kept out the weather. As Mrs. Leiter of Washington said of her Dupont Circle palace to a friend who was expatiating upon its magnificence, "Oh, well, it is a good enough shelter."

The following "tax-list was given in by E. P. Miller of Mary's Grove for 1841:"

Land—Home tract, 385 acres, worth $4,000.
Land—Underdown tract, 220 acres, $450.
Land—Mill seat and entry, 80 acres, $100.
Land—Mill tract, 30 acres, $200.
Land—Woods tract, 115 acres, $215.
Land—Braswell mine interest, 200 acres, $255.
Land—Four mountain entries, $20.
Land—Mountain land (Ashe and Caldwell), 200 acres, $220.
Yand—Clontz, Lowdermilk, Perkins and Miller, —— acres, $180.
Six (6 black polls).

Six black polls, 21 years old and over, would indicate from 25 to 30 negroes of all ages and sexes at Mary's Grove. Some of these negroes, in conjunction with other families, were engaged in road-building on the first construction of the mountain turnpike now known as the Lenoir and Blowing Rock turnpike. Maj. Miller took a contract to build one mile of this road, some distance above Mulberry Spring, and a curious incident in connection with this construction is that there is to this day, situated near the road, a clearing in a favorable southern and eastern exposure known as the "Miller Potato Patch." Raising the potatoes near the location of operafions was a provident means of furnishing the hands with this nutritious vegetable and thus doing away with that much hauling. The date of the building of this road must have been prior to 1850. Of course the record is kept by the company.

In 1899, upon the death of Mrs. W. W. Scott, only daughter of Maj. Miller, of Mary's Grove, who had eight children, black Joe Miller was greatly grieved and, in talking to a member of the family, made this affectionate remark: "There's only two of us left now—Marse Hamp and me." He referred to the late Mr. E. H. Miller—"Will Honeycombe"—and meant that they were the last of a group of children, white and black, who had been raised up together at Mary's Grove. Joe and Perry were brothers, Joe being teh youngest and Perry the oldest of their family, sons of "Mammy Tina." Both were men of high character, correct principles and of the strictest loyalty, and the writer of this counted them his dear friends for whom he had an affection as for kinsmen. The children, grandchildren and great-grandchildren of these good men may well be proud of their forbears. When Gen. Stoneman led his cavalry command of 3,000 men through Caldwell just at the close of the war they took away with them every horse and mule they could lay their hands on, and very few farmrs residing along their line of march saved any of their stock that could be taken away. Capt. N. A. Miller was absent from home with his company of Confederate cavalry, but Joe got his horses together and, with some assistance, took them to the woods. The Yankees got wind of him and trailed him, but Joe dodged from one hiding place to another, during the two or three days the raid lasted, and finally escaped; and when the coast was clear came riding home with his drove intact.

THE END

POSTSCRIPT

The preceding rambling pages do not require any preface unless it may be one to serve as an apology and to make certain additions and corrections that could not be made in the text. The "Introductory" and "Part I" carry a story. as well as it could be compiled from the material at hand, of the family of John Perkins from the date of his birth in 1733 to about 1800. This story covers the history of his sons and daughters in a fragmentary way, during that period.

"Part II" takes up the families of these children of John Perkins and is an imperfect genealogical record of these families. Such records, however complete they may be, are usually of more interest to the persons concerned than to the general public and, as might have been expected, "Part II" falls far below "Part I" in general interest and in its availability to carry anything resembling a connected story.

When it was resolved to publish these compilations in book or pamphlet form it was deemed advisable to round them out and to bring in a section that might pick up the story, temporarily laid aside when "Part I" was concluded, and carry it forward, as far as possible, along the same lines upon which "Part I" was laid. This scheme opened up the way for six or eight different associated or allied family histories, detailing manners and customs prevailing during the first half of the nineteenth century. In "Part I" John Perkins was the dominating figure. "Part III," if constructed literally upon the same lines, would have developed six or eight other dominating figures, and, if any one writer or compiler had been able to collect the material, he would have had such an embarrassment of riches in his possession as would have forced him to write several books. But no one could have entered upon such a task without preparing for years of strenuous work and tireless investigation, even if it had been possible or expedient to attempt such an extensive publishing project.

In his assiduous labor of investigating the field covered by these pages the writer has discovered that there are from six to a dozen of the allied families that would furnish, to a properly equipped writer, material for the construction of a "Part III" quite as interesting as the one herewith submitted and in a number of instances far more fascinating, considering only the material upon which the stories might be based. But if a "Part III" had to be written the one herein printed was the only one the present writer could write. because it was the only one he was entirely familiar and intimately connected with and he herewith submits it as more or less typical of the other six or eight.

The young county of Avery, except for a slight corner taken from Watauga, was a part of the old county of Burke in the days of John Perkins, and was carved out of the present counties of Burke, Caldwell, Mitchell and Watauga. Mr. William Calhoun Newland was Lieutenant-Governor of North Carolina and presiding officer of the Senate in the General Assembly of the State. The name of the county was given in honor of a family that has always been distinguished not only in Burke but in the State and nation, and of which Associate Justice of the Supreme Court Alfonso C. Avery was the leading representative at that time, the founder of the family in North Carolina having been Weightstill Avery, a Revolutionary patriot and signer of the Mecklenburg Declaration of Independence, May 20, 1775. A signal honor conferred upon the young Lieutenant-Governor and President of the Senate was the naming of the new county seat Newland. The Appalachian Training School at Boone, Watauga county, one of the most important educational institutions in the State, was always during Mr. Newland's legislative career very near to his heart, and he was very influential in establishing the school at Boone, where it is the center of a section from which it can exert its influence most advantageously. In rceognition of his unselfish service in the advancement of education in the mountains one of the great buildings of the school has been named Newland Hall.

As Col. Walton believed that Parson Miller was an Englishman and has so stated, it is but fair to the reverend pioneer to state that he was not an English, but a Lowland Scot, "born July 11, 1758, at Baldovie, near Dundee. Forfarshire (sometime Angusshire), Kingdom of North Birtain."

The "North Carolina Manual, 1874" (compiled by the late John H. Wheeler), records the following representation of Burke county in the North Carolina Senate: "1816, Alex Perkins; 1817, A. Perkins; 1818, David Tate; 1819, A. Perkins."

"Alex" Perkins, Senator in 1816, was Alexander Perkins, son of John Perkins, living on John's River.

Judge Avery says "we know that Alfred Perkins (son of Elisha and grandson of John Perkins) was Senator from Burke county in 1817. So this place sthe identity of "A. Perkins," who was Senator in 1819, in the same state of uncertainty that surrounds the question of whether the member of the House of Representatives in the Congress of 1805 was Joseph McDowell of Quaker Meadows or Joseph McDowell of Pleasant Gardens.

Page 15. Second paragraph, line 8: "The lands along this river are so well described," etc.

Page 20. Second paragraph, line 5: "63rd Congress, second session," and not 53rd.

Page 21. Line 14: "a youth as John Perkins appears," etc.

Page 30. Line 7 from the bottom: "Legislature of 1919" and not 119.

Page 32. Last paragraph: Philetus Martin's wife was Virginia Corpening.

Page 39. Lines 27 and 28: "Mrs. Mary Perkins Kent, Mrs. Emma Perkins Forney, Mrs. Elizabeth Perkins McConnaughey and Miss Susan Gordon Perkins."

Page 41. (E) Sarah Amelia: She was born in 1794 and not in 1784, as in text.

Read "Margaret Bathier" and not "Bothier." Same as to (4) next succeeding.

Page 42. Add to "(3) Mary Sumpter." etc: "There were another son and another daughter—Emma, who married Dr. Boone Clarke, son of Gen. Cornelius W. Clarke of Caldwell; Dr. Clarke was a brave Confederate soldier and a captain in the service. After the civil war they moved to Mississippi, where Dr. Clarke had an uncle living, Rev. N. L. Clarke, a brother of his father and a prominent Baptist minister. The son was Simpson Powell, a brave Confederate soldier who died in the service."

Page 49. Line 1: Read "George Fox," not "Fax."

Page 50. Line 23: Insert in blank the word "tret." Line 7, first word: Read "Edgeworth."

Page 51. "(4) Nelson Alexander Miller," etc. Add: "One daughter, Julia Sidney Miller, a beautiful character, who died unmarried."

Page 56. After "(9)" add: "(10) Cornelia married Lieut. —— Largent; married, second, P. L. Baker; children, Martha, Mrs. Bush and Miller."

Page 55. Mrs. A. A. Kent died suddenly Christmas day, 1919.

Page 58. William Macon Michaux married Martha Robinson Henderson, daughter of Lawson Pinkney and Cornelia Caldwell Henderson, granddaughter of John Caldwell, niece of the late Gov. Tod Robinson Caldwell."

Page 59. John Theodore Perkins, the eminent Burke county lawyer, died in Morganton in August, 1919, after a lingering illness.

Page 60. The initials of "Capt. H. H. Etheridge" are wrong; they should be "D. M.."

In the text there is no mention made of the first marriage of H. Theodore Newland. His first wife was Miss Katherine McDowell, daughter of the late Dr. John McDowell of Morganton. Their daughter, Margaret, is a charming young lady just budding into womanhood.

Page 61. Mrs. Robert B. Bogle's name was Martha and not Adelaide. She had four sisters, Caroline, Jane, Harriet and Adelaide. The sister Jane is mentioned in the text. Caroline and Adelaide were married and died young. Harriet died unmarried when she was 18 years old.

William G. Bogle was named William George and not William Gaither. He married Lelia McIntosh of Taylorsville, N. C., who survives, and they have a daughter and son living. The daughter married Maurice Gwaltney of Taylorsville. The son, William George Bogle, Jr., married Atlanta Gibson of South Carolina, and he is located at Columbia, S. C. During the world war he was made first lieutenant at camp and was promoted to captain and made a capable and efficient officer.

Page 62. Julius and Caleb Connelly were Confederate soldiers who died in the service. Caleb had the rank of captain and was killed at Shiloh. Their brother Harvey Perkins was also a Confederate soldier and was a United States commissioner when he died, aged 52 years. His son James is now with the Durham Hosiery Company.

Page 62. One daughter of J. Mortimer Connelly, Alice, married Mr. Gentry; the other daughter, Mary. married Mr. Creed F. Young.

Page 63. First line: Read "Ralph" instead of "Robert."

Page 64. First and second lines: It is not "Robert," but Dr. Frank E. Perkins who is prospering, not at Beunos Aires, but at Rio de Janeiro, Brazil, of the Chamber of Commerce of which city he is a member and where he has large interests.

Lines 7 and 8: The name of the daughter at home is "Cora" and not "Clara," and her sister Susie's husband is Charles R. Thomas, a druggist in Thomasville.

Page 75. First word of line 13: "Maternal" and not "material."

Page 79. Second line of second paragraph: "1790" instead of "1780."

Paragraph 4, line 2; "debt and to" and not "debt and the."

www.ingramcontent.com/pod-product-compliance
Lightning Source LLC
Chambersburg PA
CBHW080053280326

41934CB00014B/3303